SAVE! America
Your Guide to Achieving Financial Freedom

Tom Petro and Kris Messner

FOX CHASE BANK

ESTABLISHED 1867

SAVE! America: Your Guide to Achieving Financial Freedom
Tom Petro and Kris Messner

Publisher
Fox Chase Bank
4390 Davisville Road
Hatboro, PA 19040
215-682-7400
www.foxchasebank.com

Editors: Alfred and Emily Glossbrenner
Book Design/Packaging: FireCrystal Communications
Cover Design: Mayapriya Long, Bookwrights

Illustrations: The cartoons in this book originally appeared in *The New Yorker* and are used here with permission from The Cartoon Bank/Condé Nast Publications, Inc.

ISBN 978-0-9825569-3-1

Printed in the United States of America

Dedication

This book is dedicated to our dear friend Chris Oliver, who died on November 16, 1989. Chris came into our lives at a time when we needed help and guidance. He took us under his wing and showed us how we could achieve financial freedom. The principles Chris taught us have had a significant impact on our lives, and we owe a great debt of gratitude for the money lessons we learned from him. It is our privilege to share with you the concepts and ideas that he so freely shared with us so many years ago.

Acknowledgements

We are grateful for the assistance, suggestions, and input of many without whose help this book would not have been possible.

We especially thank Brigette Milligan, who provided invaluable direction and ideas, served as a cheerleader to encourage us in our work, and selected the *New Yorker* cartoons that grace these pages. Brigette was tireless in pursuing ideas and concepts to enrich the content and make the ideas useful.

We also gratefully acknowledge the contributions of our Cultural Reference Relevance Team: Dawnmarie Brigidi, Brian McGowan, Adam Regnery, Kelly Gallagher, Luke Desiato, and Christine Kontas, all of whom read the early manuscript and offered great input and feedback about how to improve the book.

We thank Bill Strecker, who was an early and ardent supporter of transforming the concepts from the book into workshop materials. And we would also like to acknowledge the invaluable contributions of Alfred and Emily Glossbrenner of FireCrystal Communications.

About the Authors

Tom Petro is president and chief executive officer of Fox Chase Bank (established in 1867). Tom serves as second vice chair of the board of the Pennsylvania Bankers Association. He is also the finance chair of the board of trustees of Eastern University and a financial services cabinet member for the United Way. Tom is a board member of the Chester County Chamber of Business and Industry.

Tom plays jazz and blues guitar, collects wines, and enjoys studying the writings of the early saints of the church. He and his wife, Kris Messner, also enjoy downhill skiing, ballroom dancing, and backcountry hiking.

LinkedIn Profile: www.linkedin.com/in/tompetro

Kris Messner is the owner of Knowledge Matters, providing business process and technology deployment consulting services to small and mid-sized businesses. Kris began her career at Mellon Bank and later consulted in bank operations and technology solutions for several of America's largest financial institutions.

Kris is the Treasurer for Surrey Services for Seniors in Berwyn, Pennsylvania, and the Treasurer and a founder of Aiding Romania's Children. She serves on the Women in Business Council for the Chester County Chamber of Business and Industry.

As a passionate road bicycler, Kris has completed over 25 "centuries" (rides of 100-miles in a single day). A talented chef, Kris is also an experienced brewmeister specializing in rather "hoppy" ales.

LinkedIn Profile: www.linkedin.com/in/krismessner

Table of Contents

Introduction

Would you like more money? Sure you would. So would we all. Well, you can have it—if you're willing to work for it. And we don't mean taking a second or third job. No, in this case, the "work" involves doing a better job of managing the income you already have.

We've presented many workshops where the word *managing* produces nothing but blank stares. And no wonder: 43% of American families spend more than they earn each year, while 42% make only the minimum credit-card payment each month.

That's not "managing." That's dogpaddling furiously to keep your head above water.

Actually, it's worse. It's really a form of slavery. Debt slavery. When all of your money goes to pay the interest on your debt, you have no room to maneuver. You can't have the things you want without adding to your debt and your interest payments. You're stuck in a ruinous debt cycle.

Put It On the Card

We know how it happens. In 1985, we were in our late 20s, living in Pittsburgh. We were newlyweds and were definitely not high flyers. In fact, we were the last among all of our friends to own a VCR. We couldn't figure out how they could afford it.

Well, it turns out that they couldn't. They ran up big credit-card bills. Or some who were in sales jobs might have had a good year and spent all their extra income on nice things.

Despite being bankers and having, as a result, a more keen awareness of money than non-bankers, we got ourselves into a situation where our credit-card debt was making us nervous.

Two quick examples illustrate how it happened. We were driving a used car, and it needed a brake job. Bang! An unexpected expense of $200. We "put it on the card."

The next month, the dishwasher suddenly stopped working. It couldn't be fixed, so we washed dishes by hand for a couple of months. But, of course, we eventually broke down and put a new dishwasher on the card.

> *"Credit is a powerful tool if used properly and an incredible slave driver if it's used incorrectly."* —Tom Petro

And so it goes. Life is expensive, and these ordinary events can happen to anyone, regardless of where they are on the economic ladder. People who are not in a position to have "new" everything have "used" everything. And used things, like used cars, wear out and break down more frequently than (most) new ones do.

That's where many people start, and it just begins to layer in, building debt (and interest due) month after month. And we haven't even included discretionary debt like choosing to eat at a fine restaurant or taking the family to Disney World. Nor have we mentioned the devastating effect of losing your job or getting hit with an enormous medical bill.

One way or another, each year millions of people find themselves in a place where the only way to get by is to max out their available credit. Once you get near that point, the burden of monthly interest reduces your financial options to zero. You can't get ahead. You can't shed this burden. You don't like being here, but you're stuck.

Yes, You Can!

One of the all-time classic movies is *The Wizard of Oz*. We've always loved the fact that Dorothy had the power to get home to Kansas all along. Had she discovered the power of her ruby slippers early on, there would have been no story. No flying monkeys. No "I'm melting! Melting!"

Well, if you're enslaved to your debt, you're like Dorothy. You have the power to break your chains—you just don't know it yet. Equally important, if you're just starting out, you have the power to avoid shackling yourself to your monthly credit-card and loan payments.

To put it another way, if you're on the "going-nowhere" treadmill, you have the power to get off. And if you're relatively young, you have the power to avoid getting on it in the first place.

How? By using the system presented in this book to *take control* of your personal finances.

Is it easy? No, it is not. Just as no diet will work unless you change your eating habits, no financial management program will work until you fundamentally change your money habits. You can't take charge of your financial life and continue to buy whatever you want whenever you want it. So, if you aren't ready to restrain such impulses, you might as well stop reading right here.

If you *are* ready, however, we have some very good news for you: Gaining financial control may be hard, but it's not as hard as you might think. And, better still, it gets easier and easier as time goes on. (Because you'll have more money!)

Developing "The System"

Ironically, we completed developing the material that led to this book on the Fourth of July, Independence Day. Our sources were our own experience, of course, and the wonderful guidance we got from Chris Oliver, our financial counselor back in Pittsburgh.

From the beginning, we agreed that the system had to be genuinely "do-able." No absolutely drastic changes. Just a few important changes around the margins. We knew from personal experience that even marginal changes, if you stick with them over time, can produce significant results.

Small Changes, Big Results

For example, ask yourself what you pay for a cup of coffee when you stop in at WaWa, Dunkin Donuts, Starbucks, or some other place on your way to work. Multiply that figure by the number of workdays in a month. Then compare it to what you'd pay at a store like Walmart or Costco to buy in bulk (coffee, cups, and lids).

We think you'll be amazed (as we were) at the available savings. So, yes, we brew our own coffee at home and take it with us before we head out for our jobs.

The point is that we haven't given up "commuter coffee." We've just found a less expensive way to buy this small, optional pleasure. (Or in Tom's case, required "caffeine fix.")

That's the kind of marginal change we're talking about.

As another example, consider a working couple's need for two cars. The natural instinct if you have only one car is to buy a second one and take on a second car payment. Thanks to Chris Oliver's sage advice, however, we didn't do that. Instead we sucked it up and took turns driving each other to and from work—all the while energetically saving for a second car.

At the end of four years, we had enough money saved to buy a second car—and to pay *cash* for it. No loan. No debt. No interest. And no car payment.

This is not "the impossible dream." We're just like you, and, applying the system you'll learn about here, we did it.

Financial Freedom

The best way to imagine financial freedom for yourself is to add up the non-mortgage debt payments you must make for one month. Look at the total and imagine what it would feel like to have that much money each month to use any way you please. Saving for college or for a new car. Taking the family on a trip. Buying new clothes and shoes. Anything. And the next month, you get to do it again.

Financial freedom means having choices. Choices you don't have right now because you must pay so much of your income to the credit-card companies. And you get nothing for it other than a moment of instant gratification.

You're not even getting the use of the money, since it's already been spent and exchanged for "stuff" you thought you wanted (but are probably now tired of having).

Frightening Facts About Credit Cards

- The typical credit-card purchase ends up costing 112% *more* than if you'd paid cash. So a $100 credit-card purchase actually costs $212.

- If you make only the minimum payment due on your credit card, it will take you 22 years to pay off your balance in full.

- According to *Forbes* magazine (2009), the average credit-card debt for each American household is $9,797.

Getting control of your finances and gaining financial freedom also means having the chance to fulfill your dreams. Remember, a fantasy is something you can think about, but a *dream is something you can achieve.* Having financial freedom makes dreams possible.

But you've got to have a goal, a plan, and apply persistent action and hard work. Achievement, it is said, is the result of laboring greatly, over an extended period of time, in the same direction. And, of course, like all journeys this one begins with a single step—laying out your Master Plan.

Your Master Plan

We've given it a grand name, but a Master Plan is essentially just a list of clear objectives. They can be short-term, medium-term, or long-term. Or a mixture of all three. These are the things that you're striving for. They're the dreams that become possible as you gain more and more financial freedom.

Here are some examples you might want to consider:

- I want to build a "rainy-day" fund to cover my expenses for three to six months, so that I can sleep at night if I lose my job.

- I want to stop paying so much of my income for interest. So I plan to pay off all my loans and credit cards.

- Then I want to start making extra payments on my mortgage loan. (The interest you can save by paying off mortgage loans early is simply amazing.)

- To make sure I have a comfortable retirement, once I've got the rainy-day fund built up, I want to save 10% of my after-tax income for retirement in a 401(k) and IRA.

- I want a child-free vacation at the Atlantis Resort in the Bahamas.

- I want to remodel my kitchen.

Non-Financial Master Plan Goals

Of course, your Master Plan goals do not have to be exclusively financial. In his book, *The Dream Manager*, Matthew Kelly identifies twelve areas to explore for setting goals for your Master Plan, along with examples of each one:

1. **Physical**   Run a marathon.
Look and feel healthy.

2. **Emotional**   Buy my own home.
Be in a great relationship.

3. **Intellectual**   Go back to school.
Learn another language.

4. **Spiritual**   Develop greater inner peace.
Study Scripture.

5. **Psychological** Strengthen my will power.
Overcome a fear of heights or flying.

6. **Material**   Get a new car.
Put a new roof on the house.

7. **Professional**   Get a promotion.
Become the best at what I do.

8. **Financial**   Pay off all credit card debt.
Start a college fund for my children.

9. **Creative**   Write a book.
Take a painting course.

10. **Adventure**   Visit Australia.
See U2 live in concert.

11. **Legacy**   Volunteer for my favorite charity.
Raise my children with a healthy sense of who they are.

12. **Character**   Develop more patience.
Do what I say I will.

We encourage you to explore a broader array of your dreams when putting together your Master Plan. (To learn more about Matthew Kelly's ideas for setting Master Plan goals, visit www.thedreammanager.com.) But remember that the key to fulfilling your dreams is to gain financial freedom.

Imagine how good it will feel having that rainy-day fund to fall back on. Imagine how relaxed you'll be, knowing you can pay your bills without going into debt. Imagine an end to the stress of dealing with bill collectors.

Finally, imagine how much more you'll enjoy your vacation or new kitchen knowing that it's paid for. Imagine the joy that will be yours when your good financial fitness allows you the freedom to explore your larger life dreams.

The Road Map to Financial Freedom

There has always been a close relationship between time and money. For example, if you start saving for retirement early in time, your money will have more time to grow. If you don't start until you're 45, you'll never be able to match the returns of someone who began at 25. And, if you relentlessly pay off debt, the amount of money you free up to spend on other things will grow over time.

Nothing about saving money is ever quick. But time and money are a powerful combination. If you're diligent and patient, you'll be amazed at what is possible.

You didn't get into debt instantly. It took time. It's logical that it will take you time to get out of debt. Most people should figure on two to three years. And no, that doesn't mean living on just bread and water in the years to come.

But gaining financial freedom *does* mean changing the way you live, starting with how you think about money. That's why the next section of this book is called "Money Myths."

That's followed by the "7 Principles of Financial Freedom." This is your road map. This is "the system," and we'll show you how to make it work in your own life. We'll show you how to manage your credit and how to become a saver.

Overview of the 7 Principles

The Principles of Financial Freedom shown nearby are not numbered randomly. They actually form a sequence of steps that build upon each other. In other words, it's important to do things in the right order.

First, you make a budget. That will help you see, possibly for the first time in your adult life, where the money's going.

7 Principles of Financial Freedom

#1: Make a budget and stick to it.

#2: Give yourself an allowance.

#3: Restrict the use of your debit card.

#4: Establish "cash-reserve" accounts.

#5: Start paying off your debts.

#6: Pay yourself first.

#7: Live within your means.

Next, you give yourself a cash allowance and make it a line item on your budget. This is not an obvious step, but it's important because it's a convenient way to gain control of what you spend on things like commuter coffee, vending machine snacks, beer and pizza with your co-workers, movies, and things like that.

You go to the ATM for cash once on payday, and that's it until your next payday. You can spend the money on anything you want. But when it's gone, it's gone—until you get paid again.

The same concept applies to the next principle: Restricting the use of your debit card. You do this by limiting its use to groceries and gasoline. No more card swipes to pay for doughnuts at the WaWa or 7-11. That comes out of your cash allowance.

You might think that paying off your high-interest credit cards would be the next step, but it's not. The next step is to start building up targeted "cash-reserve" funds while continuing to pay the minimums on your cards.

Cash-reserve funds can be aimed at anything you like. But here are some helpful suggestions:

- Automobile Repairs and Inspections

- Clothing for Work

- Home Repairs and Appliances

- Vacations and Fun (Very important.)

- Tuition and Books

The goal is to build these funds up so that you never have to use your credit card to pay for these things. That's how you get off the credit-card-debt treadmill.

"You want to find things that are not terribly painful to do without in your life, to free up the cash you need to start your cash-reserve accounts." –Kris Messner

Once you've built robust cash-reserve accounts, you can start paying off your debt, starting with the card or loan carrying the highest interest rate.

Pay off your debts, then start "paying yourself first." That means putting aside money for your retirement.

Finally, and you should start doing this right away, "Live within your means." In fact, you should try to live *below* your means. Pay cash for almost everything, and spend less of it than you actually have.

"But I Don't Have Any Extra Money"

We get that a lot. We respond by making two points. First, the more money you can put into your cash-reserve accounts, the better. But it doesn't have to be a huge amount. If you have five accounts and can put $10 into each of them each pay period, for a total of $50, you'll be surprised at how that can add up.

Second, everyone can find extra money to fund these accounts. Everyone. You just have to focus your attention on your spending and be willing to make a few tweaks. Seriously. If you apply yourself, you can probably find anywhere from $50 to $200 in "extra cash" each month.

Looking for Savings

Our friend, Joan, gave us a good example of what's possible. Before the "Great Recession" of 2007-2009, Joan made a nice living as a successful real-estate agent. Then she saw most of her income disappear as the real-estate market froze.

So, she began cutting costs.

Joan has a big-box freezer in her garage. She emptied and unplugged it. She raised all of her thermostats in the summer by about 8 degrees to save money on air conditioning. (She used a fan instead.)

Then she went around the house and unplugged many of the appliances that suck up electricity even when they are "off." (They're called electricity "vampires.")

She stopped going to restaurants and began making all her meals at home. She started batching her automobile errands to save on gas.

She then shifted her wardrobe so that she wears things she can wash instead of things that need to be dry-cleaned. She's closed the forced-air registers in rooms she doesn't use.

All of these actions have helped her significantly reduce her cost of living.

Joan was forced to do this because she was essentially out of work. Imagine what extra cash someone who has a steady paycheck could find by taking similar steps in his or her home.

The truth is that you have all kinds of extra money; you just have to look at how you're using it. You only have to make changes on the margins to substantially affect your financial future.

Why heat or cool an unoccupied room? Why leave all the lights on? Why go out to lunch every day when you could easily "brown-bag it" several days a week? (It would probably be better for both your wallet and your waistline!)

Even More Ways to Save!

For more money-saving ideas, please see "Principle 7: Live Within Your Means" later in this book. Once you get into the swing of things, it's amazing how many expenses you can cut without reducing your quality of life.

Celebration Points: Milestones and Rewards

We have saved the best part of the system for last. Namely *rewards*. If you have established and stuck with the system, giving yourself a reward when you reach a certain milestone does no harm at all. In fact, doing so can go a long way toward encouraging your continued success.

So, when you reach the milestone of completely paying off your highest-interest credit card, give yourself a reward. Go out to dinner with your significant other. Buy yourself the pair of shoes or power tool, or take on one of the non-financial goals that's been on your wish list.

Just be sure to pay cash!

The Way Forward

Finally, here comes the carrot and the stick. The stick is that if you do not take action now, you'll continue to be miserable. You'll continue to be chained to the debt treadmill. And in the future, it will only be worse.

The carrot is that being debt-free is a great place to be. Many people have been enslaved by debt for so long that they can no longer imagine what it's like to have real financial freedom and choices.

We are living proof that this can be done. *You can do this.* But you've got to start. You've got to take that first step: Changing the way you think about money. That's what we'll cover next in "Money Myths." What you learn there is sure to surprise you.

Money Myths

There's a silent black-and-white comedy video of a film dating from the early 1900s showing various men attempting to fly. They strap on homemade wings or get into other contraptions and literally take a flying leap, flapping madly. Inevitably, they end up crashing into a heap at the bottom of a cliff or at the end of a ramp.

Why would they do this? In the absence of any scientific testing of their equipment and with no evidence that their devices would work, they attempted to fly anyway. (And they invited photographers to film them!)

We know the answer. They did it because of what they *believed*. They really believed that if they flapped their balsa wings fast enough, they could fly.

> *"The aphorism, 'As a man thinketh in his heart, so is he,' not only embraces the whole of a man's being, but is so comprehensive as to reach out to every condition and circumstance of his life."*
> —James Allen, *As a Man Thinketh*

Here's an example of something we all know to be true but rarely apply in our lives: Beliefs drive behavior, and behavior drives results.

To put it another way, what you believe about money and your financial life directly impacts how you handle that money and how you manage your financial life. It is simple human nature.

But what if your beliefs about money are wrong? Let's take it a step further: What if it turns out that everything you think you know about money and your relationship to money is untrue?

How can you possibly break the chains of debt slavery if what you believe about money is basically a lie? (That may be too strong, so let's just say it's "false.") Or at least it is for a lot of people.

10 Money Myths

We're going to have a lot more to say about this topic in a moment. For the time being, take a look at these 10 Money Myths and see if any of them apply to you:

1. All my money problems would go away if I made more money.

2. My present financial condition is because of things outside my control.

3. Money has value in and of itself.

4. I spend my money based on my needs.

5. Going into debt opens up choices for me now instead of having to wait until later.

6. I know where I spend my cash.

7. My checkbook balance is a good indicator of my financial situation.

8. I can't afford to plan for my retirement.

9. Sticking to a budget limits my freedom of choice.

10. Two people can live more cheaply than one.

The Catalyst

If you're going to gain financial freedom, you've got to change the way you think about money. If we can achieve that, then this part of the book will have done its job.

But before we move on, it's important for you, our readers, to have some idea of how this book, and the series of workshops that preceded it, came to be.

Let Tom tell the tale:

Kris and I are both bankers. But what prompted us to write this book was finding out that one of my employees had to go out and secure a "payday loan"—a small, short-term loan with very high fees—to pay his bills.

It broke my heart in so many ways. But it was mostly that one of the people that I care deeply about, someone who was part of our own bank family, was having so much money stress that he had to use a payday loan to get by.

It spoke to me on many different levels. As the CEO of the company, I knew that we work very hard to pay our people competitive wages and to provide good health and educational benefits. Yet all the work we do to care for our folks was insufficient in the case of this individual employee.

An Interest Rate of 304%!

We recently saw a TV ad for a payday loan. A very pleasant spokesperson said, "Got 'the shorts' between now and your next payday? No problem. We'll loan you $300 to get through the next 10 days. And the cost is just $25. If the loan helps you avoid just one over-draft fee, it will have paid for itself. Come see us today! You've got nothing to lose!"

But you do have something to lose, of course. The $25 fee works out to an annual interest rate of 304%. Anyone who opts for such a loan is obviously intent on solving a very immediate problem, like paying the rent. But what happens the next time?

It also troubled me to think, "We're bankers, and if we're not expert at managing our own money, then how in the world can we ever carry out our job of helping other people do the same thing?"

So I decided it was crucial to share what Kris and I know from our own personal financial-management experience with employees of Fox

Chase Bank, many of whom already know these principles, but some of whom do not. It's not an exaggeration to say that the whole thing just poured out of me.

Then I passed it to Kris, and she made many important contributions, edits, and improvements. And so the workshops we offer to bank employees and to members of our community were born. And now we've captured it all in this book so we can reach an even wider audience.

The two of us feel passionately about this "mission," and we are so grateful to have gotten good advice so early in our careers. We want to give others the same gift.

Exploding the Myths About Money

Now, let's take a look at each of these 10 myths in turn and seek out the truth. The results may surprise you.

Myth #1: All my money problems would go away if I made more money.

This is the most insidious money myth of all. It's hard to get your arms around it because everyone tends to think, "I'm just one pay raise away from being in good financial shape." Or, "All I need is a promotion and a 10% raise, then I'll be fine."

If you're honest with yourself, you know that isn't going to happen. If you look back, you probably said the exact same thing before each of your last five pay raises.

So where did the extra money go? Inflation? Sure. But we all know the truth:

The more we make, the more we spend.

We know a lot of people, for instance, who live in million-dollar homes. But because they've spent all their salary increases (and then some), they have no furniture. They have no free money.

It doesn't matter where you are on the income ladder: Spending *always* increases with income unless spending habits are brought under control.

So, if you're waiting for your next pay raise to be able to make ends meet, we hate to be the bearer of bad news: You will never arrive. You will never get there. And deep in your heart, you know it.

The spending bar keeps moving higher and higher with our rising income. The more we make, the more we spend.

More money won't solve your problems. You need to take control of the money you're already making.

Myth #2: My present financial condition is because of things outside my control.

For some of us, it's a very hard truth to accept, but the fact is, even though we may not exercise it, each of us has control over our financial situation.

That's what our friend Ben was doing as he wrote the check for his last car payment. He planned to keep the "expenditure" in his budget, but instead of it going for the car loan, he'd put a third of the amount into his rainy-day fund and apply another third to accelerate payments against his credit-card debt. The remaining third would be used to boost his cash allowance and add to his "fun" account.

He figured that having paid off his car loan, he'd earned the right to visit Seattle's Best once or twice a week on his increased allowance. And he and his wife planned to spend a weekend in Myrtle Beach to celebrate paying off the loan.

Ben put the car-payment check in the mail.

Two days later, he was rear-ended by an uninsured driver. Thankfully, he wasn't injured, but the car was totaled.

Because it was an older car, the Kelley Blue Book value wasn't very high. Ben had taken good care of his car, and he had expected to be able to drive it for five or six more years—years that would be car-payment-free. The car was thus worth far more to Ben than its book value.

The settlement check was pretty lousy—far less than what it would take to replace that car. So Ben would need another car loan. And, of course, because the other driver was uninsured, the payment came from *his* insurance company, so his policy's deductible was subtracted from the amount of the check.

"We are solely responsible for how we spend our money. We control the choices we make along the way that determine how well prepared we are for the unexpected."—Tom Petro

Bad things *do* happen, things over which we have no control. Being rear-ended by an uninsured driver is pretty close to the top of the list. Having your dishwasher or refrigerator die may be a notch or two lower on the pain meter, but it is still not a trivial event.

But none of this changes the fact that we are solely responsible for how we spend our money. We control the choices we make along the way that determine how well prepared we are for the unexpected. No one else but you is accountable for the financial choices you make.

Think about this for a moment. How do you spend your money? What are you using your money for? Every choice you make is driven by your system of beliefs about money. If you think your financial situation is hopeless, if you believe your financial path is outside of your control, you will make wrong choices about how to use your money.

Your wrong choices will lead you further into debt and further into a place of hopelessness and despair. But if you accept accountability for how you spend your money, you will find that you can take charge of your finances, make consistently good choices, and discover the path to financial freedom.

By changing your incorrect beliefs about money, you can take charge of your financial situation and be prepared when the unexpected financial disruption comes into your life.

Change and Motivation

If you don't take control, who will? That paycheck is made out to you and no one else. Do it for yourself, for your kids, for your life partner. There's nothing more debilitating to a relationship than money problems. When both people get on the same page regarding a plan and are working toward a common objective, it actually builds intimacy in the relationship.

Myth #3: Money has value in and of itself.

Gold and silver (and copper and nickel, for that matter) have value as metals because you can add them to products or otherwise make something out of them. But they have *no intrinsic value* as money. Nor does paper money.

The reason money of any sort "works" is that everyone is willing to exchange it for goods and services. Some of those goods and services may have value. Some may not. Some may be just "stuff."

Money, of course, is a substitute for time. We trade our time for money every day. And we buy time whenever we hire someone to mow the lawn or baby-sit or clean the gutters. We trade our time doing what we do well to pay others for doing what they do well—things we could never do in a million years, like changing out a transmission.

"I'm putting all my money into 'things.'"

It is our *time* that is precious, not our money. After all, none of us ever gets enough time. It is not elastic, meaning that it does not increase with demand. No matter how many days you want, you will only get the number allotted to you. So how you spend them matters.

That's what retirement is really all about. Everybody has the same choice: You can choose to live paycheck-to-paycheck, spending everything you make, or you can choose to store up money (time) to be used in the future.

Can you retire at 55? Sure you can—if you start planning and saving for it when you are much younger. We have a friend, Jim, who did exactly that. He's 60 now, and he spends the time he saved for on the things he enjoys—volunteering at the hospital and church, playing with his grandchildren, and traveling the world with his wife.

He can do all this because when he was 25 or so, he set a goal of retiring at 55. He created a financial plan, and he stuck to it.

Now our friend enjoys the fruits of financial discipline while other people his age are having to work 10 or 20 more years before they retire, if they can ever retire at all. By creating and sticking to a financial plan, Jim now trades his money for time—time to do the things that he really wants to do in life.

Money has no value in and of itself. It only can be exchanged for things of value—or for time.

Myth #4: I spend my money based on my needs.

No you don't! Like all of us, you spend your money based on your *wants*. And advertising agencies on Madison Avenue and elsewhere are being paid a lot of money to constantly create those wants and dangle them in front of you.

Open the door to your garage and take a look. How many items in there do you still use? Almost by definition, if they're in the garage, you or a family member has tired of them and put them out to pasture.

But here's the irony: Fully 70% of the American economy is based on consumer spending. So, if you don't do your part and trade a major portion of your time on this earth for things you want but don't really need, the economy will falter.

That being the case, is it any wonder that so much effort is expended to persuade you to buy, say, some kind of food dicer or slicer when you already have a food processor with a complete set of blades and disks?

We all know the truth: Emotions drive our spending habits, not real needs. That's why we buy the $95 shirt or blouse when the $35 version would do just fine. It's why the kids simply must have the $150 athletic shoes instead of the $40 pair.

We're not saying don't buy what you want. We're saying just stop and think before you whip out your wallet and "put it on the card."

Consider Your Car

Here's an even bigger example. You need a car to get to work. No question about that. But do you need—really *need*—a brand-new car? (Brand-new cars lose 30% of their resale value as soon as you drive them off the lot.) We definitely don't want to sound like your parents, but please think about it.

As we write this, a brand-new Acura TSX lists for about $29,000 (5-speed automatic or 6-speed manual). It is one cool car, no doubt about it. On the other hand, a year-old "pre-owned" Toyota Camry LE lists for $17,400.

"Tom and I know that our readers aren't going to stop buying stuff, any more than we are. The key is to get everyone to free up just 2% to 5% of their take-home money to accelerate debt repayment and build cash-reserve accounts. It is quite do-able. We're not suggesting you need to save half your paycheck." –Kris Messner

They will both get you to work in style, but the price difference is $11,600. And that's just the spread between the "list" prices. If you do your homework, you can almost certainly get the used car for a lower price, while there may be less dealer flexibility on the brand-new car.

Here's the kicker. If you buy the brand-new Acura and finance it with a four-year loan at 5.2%, you will pay $268 per month *more* than if you bought the pre-owned year-old Camry. In other words, repaying that extra $11,600 will cost you $12,864 ($11,600 plus $1,264 in interest).

For many people, cars are about much more than basic transportation. All we're saying is that before you go for the hot new car you want, step back and think about what this indulgence (and, yes, it is definitely an indulgence) will really cost. Then ask yourself, "Is it truly worth it to me?" And then ask yourself, "What can I cut back on or do without to be able to pay for it?"

Dealing with "Indulgences"

Plays by the ancient Greeks, and later, the Romans, often promoted the theme of "all things in moderation." Wine? Of course, but with the proper, moderate, dilution with water. Women, well, let's not go there. The point was, "Everything in balance."

As Tom readily admits, a few years ago, his addiction to music CDs was approaching the "Out of Control" line. (Tom is a jazz guitarist who has a huge enthusiasm for any kind of music.)

Recognizing the problem, we set up a new procedure. Now Tom empties his pocket change into a dish at the end of each day. When the dish is full (it takes about three months), we take the coins to the grocery store and dump them into the coin counter.

But instead of opting for folding money, we opt for iTunes points. So we can buy downloadable music from that site. You can also get "e-cert" numbers for online merchants that include Amazon, Borders, CVS, JCPenney, Lowe's, and Starbucks. And, if you chose any non-cash option, you don't pay the 8% for the automatic sorting.

Myth #5: Going into debt opens up choices for me now instead of having to wait until later.

Taking out a loan to start a business does indeed have the *potential* to open up choices for you in the future. But that's not what most people mean when they recite this myth. What they mean is going into debt by using their credit cards to buy what they want *now* instead of saving for what they want and paying cash for it *later*.

The promise of instant gratification is what makes credit cards so seductive. And yet, what do we all buy with them? Anyone who has strolled around a residential neighborhood in summer, when the garage doors are open, knows the answer. We buy "stuff." So much stuff that there is no longer room to park the cars in the garage. (For a humorous, but profanity-laced, monologue on "stuff," visit YouTube.com and do a search on "George Carlin" and "stuff." It is one of the late comedian's classic performances.)

Your Future in Perspective

Borrowing money means that you have to use part of your future income to pay back what you owe. This means you will have less money to spend on what you want in the future. You will thus have *less*, not more, freedom of choice.

Look at this month's credit-card bills and ask yourself, "If I only paid cash for what I bought, how much of my paycheck would I be free to spend on things today?" Your answer will ultimately be determined by decisions you made a year or more ago.

Today is the "now" that was your future back then, and you are living with the aftermath of the financial decisions you made at that time.

Credit provides the illusion of freedom of choice right "now," today. After all, who can resist the ads that shout, "No payments for 24 months"? It's seductive to believe that we can have it now and pay for it later without any additional costs or consequences.

Just a Dollar Down and a Dollar a Week!

 The revolving-credit problem for American consumers didn't begin with our generation. It clearly dates at least as far back as the 1920s. That's when big-ticket items, like refrigerators, began to be sold like automobiles—on credit.

Before that, buying on credit was considered somewhat shameful. The folksinger Woody Guthrie captured it all in his song, later made famous by The Limelighters, *A Dollar Down and a Dollar a Week*. "A Dollar a Week" is the old-time equivalent of the "minimum monthly payment" on your credit card bill. That number often doesn't seem too bad when you're considering a purchase.

But let's look more closely at the fine print. Your monthly credit-card payment includes both a **principal payment**, which reduces what you owe, and an **interest payment**.

The minimum principal payment differs with every card, but it's generally between 2% and 4% of the outstanding balance. So let's say your outstanding balance is $8,000, the minimum principal repayment is 2%, and the interest rate is 19%. Your minimum payment for the month will be $286.67.

Don't worry about working out the arithmetic right now. We've already done it for you here, and we'll explain the details in a later section. The key point is this: Of that $286.67 monthly payment, $160 will go toward paying down your principal, while $126.67 will go for interest.

What you won't find in the fine print is far more discouraging: If you only pay the minimum each month, it will take you 22 years to pay everything off. And by the way, this assumes that you won't be putting any more charges on your credit card for the next two decades.

But there *are* consequences. As anyone who is buried beneath a mountain of credit-card debt knows all too well. Credit-card debt is a terrible hole. And we don't just stumble into it. We choose to walk into it, and the path leads deeper and deeper over time. The problem is that once you're deep in debt, it can be very difficult to escape.

We're going to show you how to do it, but first we've got to continue exploding myths.

Myth #6: I know where I spend my cash.

We'd like to suggest that you do *not* know where you spend your cash.

Here's a quick reality check. Think about, say, a week ago Thursday. Where did you spend your money or swipe your debit or credit card? How much was the gasoline fill-up? Did you remember the dry cleaner? What about the pizza slice you picked up or the bottled water you bought from the vending machine?

You can't remember, can you? That's not some kind of mental defect. None of us can remember.

A cup of coffee here, a candy bar there, a newsstand magazine, a box of cookies from some charitable organization's fund drive—there's no way to remember everything. But it still all adds up.

That's why, as we'll discuss later when we get to the "Principles of Financial Freedom," giving yourself a cash allowance is so important. It frees you from ever having to record each and every daily expenditure. It's simple: You can spend your allowance on anything you want. But when it's gone, it's gone until your next payday.

Myth #7: My checkbook balance is a good indicator of my financial situation.

Automated Teller Machines (ATMs) have been placed in convenience stores for decades. But it is only when we began helping people visualize the path to financial freedom that we began to notice a particular human behavior.

We'd be standing in line at the check-out counter and see someone go up to the ATM, put in his card, tap the screen, and pull out a receipt a moment later. The individual would look at it and either put it in his pocket or toss it into the trash. These folks never withdrew any cash.

Bankers that we are, we wondered, "What's going on?"

It turns out that these people, most of them young, were checking their account balance to see how much fun they could have during the coming weekend. Do I have enough in my checking account to go to the Eagles game? Can I take my girlfriend out to dinner at that restaurant on Two Street, or do we have to dial it down a bit? In other words, "What's my current financial situation?"

You kind of want to drench them with a bucket of ice water in hopes of waking them up. Hello! A checking account balance tells you how much you have *left* to spend, not what you're going to *need* to spend. Which includes "minor" things like your rent, your car payment, health and auto insurance, credit-card debt... the list goes on. Not to mention, unplanned expenses like car repairs, household appliance repairs, and disposing of a tree that was felled by last week's thunderstorm that also took out your electric power.

Here's the bottom line: If your checkbook is your only financial-management tool, you're in big trouble.

Myth #8: I can't afford to plan for my retirement.

The fact is, you can't afford *not* to plan for your retirement. If you retire at 65, statistically, you could easily have another 20 years to live. You should figure that you'll need between 70% and 100% of your former salary to maintain your current lifestyle in retirement.

Where's the money going to come from? Social Security? Many people aren't aware of this, but Social Security is designed to cover only about 40% of the income you'll need in retirement.

Again, where's the other 60% going to come from? Unless you're in line for a big inheritance, it can only come from your own savings and investments.

You might be saying, "Who cares? I'm just starting out. Retirement is a long way off."

That's precisely the point. In all likelihood, you're going to need hundreds of thousands of dollars in savings to be able to retire in comfort. The only way to amass that kind of retirement fund is to start saving *now*.

When it comes to money, if you think you have it bad now, you cannot imagine the future hell that is waiting for you, courtesy of your wrong thinking and incorrect beliefs about money. "Who cares?" you say. That future is a long way off. Precisely. That's why it's so important to plan right now.

Taking Advantage of Compound Interest

There's a very practical reason to begin immediately. It's called the "Miracle of Compound Interest," and it simply means earning interest on the interest you've earned in the past.

For example, suppose you're 25, and you invest $1,000 in a mutual fund IRA that earns an average of 8% a year. At that rate, your money will double every nine years. By the time you're 65, that $1,000 will have become $32,000.

If you wait until you turn 26 to start investing $1,000 a year, you'll have just cost yourself $32,000 in retirement savings.

Please, pause to contemplate this. Time and money. It is such a powerful "iron law," that delaying by even a single year can cost you big time when you're ready to retire. Who knows what the cool cars will cost when you retire, but an extra $32,000 has to help. And when you retire, if you've been smart about saving and investing, you can treat yourself to a brand-new car, knowing full well how much it drops in value when you drive it off the lot. It's okay. You've worked for it, and you deserve it.

Another way of referring to the "Miracle of Compound Interest" is "the time value of money." It is because of this that you can't wait until you pay off your credit cards to start saving for retirement.

Make time work *for* you and start putting some money, no matter how small the amount, into a tax-deferred retirement account today. At the very least you should strive to get the maximum available match from your employer's 401(k) plan.

The Latte Millionaire Plan

Several years ago, financial columnist Scott Burns introduced a concept he called the "Margarita Millionaire Plan" to explain how you could accumulate a million dollars by retirement if you gave up and salted away the money you'd save by giving up just one margarita a day. He recently updated the idea to substitute a latte for the margarita.

Here's how it works: If your latte habit costs about $3.50 a day, that's $24.50 a week, $105 a month, and $1,277.50 a year. Assuming that at age 25 you begin investing that sum each year in a simple domestic stock index earning a long-term average of 10%, by the time you reach 67, what Burns calls the "Latte Growth Fund" will total $983,614, or close to a million dollars.

That's the power of compound interest over time, in this case 42 years of saving just $3.50 a day.

Myth #9: Sticking to a budget limits my freedom of choice.

There's this false notion that if you have a budget, it restricts you and takes away your freedom. After all, a budget takes choice away, doesn't it?

Many people wrongly conclude, "If something I want is not in my budget, then by sticking to my budget I can't have what I want. That would seem to limit my choice."

The truth is, a budget actually *gives* you freedom. It empowers you. Once you begin to take control and actually plan how you're going to spend your money, you end up with more money left over that you can actually spend the way you want to. That's real freedom.

Developing and sticking to a budget gives you more control over the important choices in your life.

The Benefits of Having a Financial Road Map

Would you get in your car and drive to San Diego without a road map or GPS system to help you navigate? Probably not. So why does it somehow make sense to go through your life without a financial road map to help you make wise choices about your money?

The late management guru and author, Peter Drucker, once said, "If you cannot measure it, you cannot manage it." Clearly, if you want to take charge of your financial affairs and put yourself on the road to financial freedom, you need a way to measure how you use your money. You need a budget.

A budget is a financial road map. It's a tool that helps you make correct choices so you can go from living paycheck to paycheck to a place of financial freedom. Without this kind of financial road map, like every one of us, you'll simply be driven by impulse to spend, spend, spend. And do you know what you'll buy? Things you want today but won't care about tomorrow.

We are slaves to our impulses and self-driven wants. Slaves are not free. Slaves are captives. We are often financial captives to our poor financial choices until we decide to make better choices with our money. But sticking to a budget can fix all that. It is the path to financial freedom.

Myth #10: Two people can live more cheaply than one.

In a subtle way, this final "Money Myth" is a variation on the very first myth, "If I only had more money...."

Here's where the fallacy lies: Clearly, if two people with jobs move in together, each will have lower monthly expenses. That's because they will each be paying half the mortgage or rent and half of the utility bills.

The problem is that when you both have more discretionary money, you'll each *spend* that extra money. (You know you will!)

The only way two people can live more cheaply than one is if they mutually agree on their financial priorities and develop a joint plan to reach their financial goals, including a joint budget. Otherwise, with competing financial priorities, the two will dig a deeper financial hole together than either of them would individually.

A moment ago, we spoke of the power of compound interest. Well, combine that with what's possible when two people with jobs share not only expenses but also priorities, and you'll not only guarantee a comfortable retirement, you'll both arrive at true financial freedom faster than you would have ever dreamed possible.

The Next Step

It's our hope that we've helped you change the way you think about money by exploding these ten insidious myths. We cannot say it too often: Beliefs drive actions, and actions determine results. And, when it comes to breaking the chains of credit-card debt and achieving financial freedom, the most important belief of all is: I can do this!

Yes you can! And as we next turn to the "7 Principles of Financial Freedom," we're going to show you exactly how.

Principle 1:
Make a Budget
and Stick to It

To paraphrase the Peter Drucker quote we discussed in the Introduction, if you can't measure your spending, you can't control it. For example, how many times did you go to the ATM last month? How much cash did you take out each time? And where did that money go? Did you buy gasoline or groceries? Movie or sports-event tickets?

You get the point. For all too many of us, the money just "goes." And we can't remember how we spent it. A budget is designed to fix that problem.

Now, some people tend to think of going on a budget like going on a diet. They think they'll have to give up a lot of things to make it work. In other words, it'll be painful.

But that's really not the case. Far from being painful, having a budget to plan your expenses will make you feel good, because being in control of your finances feels good. You can still have the things you want, but you won't have to go into debt and shoulder more interest payments to do so. (Remember, interest payments can go on seemingly forever, and you don't get anything for them.)

Making a budget is the first step on the road to financial freedom. So let's get started.

Gathering What You'll Need

You'll need a calculator, a pencil or pen, and access to either a photocopier or an Internet-equipped computer and printer.

In the Appendix section of this book, you'll find a detailed budget template that you can photocopy. Or you can visit the Fox Chase Bank Web site (www.foxchasebank.com) and download the same template as an Excel worksheet, a Microsoft Word document (.doc) file, or an Adobe PDF file.

To access the files, click on "SAVE! America" in the "Special Offers for You!" section. As we work through this section of the book, we're going to assume that you have either a photocopy or a printout of that budget template near at hand.

Budgeting On-disk and Online

Quicken Deluxe Software ($60) is undoubtedly the best-selling personal finance manager. And, of course, it has a budget-making module. If you aren't sure you want to purchase new software, you can also use online tools, some of which are free. Leading sites include Yodlee, Quicken Online, and Mint.com (now owned by Quicken's parent, Intuit).

You'll have to supply these sites with the information they need to access your bank account to download bank transactions. Fox Chase Bank's Direct Connect, interfaces directly with Quicken and QuickBooks.

Next, you'll need your bank statements, checkbook register, and credit-card statements for the last three months. You could get started by collecting just one month's worth of statements, but there's always a chance that you'll miss some expense that you pay quarterly or several times a year instead of monthly.

Your budget doesn't have to be perfect the first time through. The important thing is to make a start. Start building a "foundation document" that you'll add to and otherwise modify as time goes on.

Where Did the Money Go?

Before you begin in earnest—and before you look at your financial papers—fill in what you *think* you spend on each item on the budget template. Then print out a second copy and start filling in the *actual* amounts, based on your statements and checkbook register.

You know what comes next: Compare the two "budgets." Where are there differences between what you *think* you're spending and what you're *actually* spending? Are there categories where you spend significantly more than what you thought you did? Does how your money was actually spent reflect how you would have *chosen* to spend your money, if you had thought about it in advance? The answers may come as a surprise. So *that's* where the money really went!

Now you're ready to get down to business. We're going to assume that you've filled out a copy of the budget template as accurately as possible. There should be a dollar figure in the Total column for every budget item that applies to you and your household.

Next, add all of the figures in the Total column and compare the sum to your monthly income. (If you're using three months of financial statements, then use three months of income.) If your expenses are lower than your income, you're ahead of the game already. If not, you've got some tough work to do. That's what we'll talk about next.

Making Budget Cuts

See the three "Cut" columns on the template? Every item on your budget falls into one of those three categories:

- **Can't Cut** (nondiscretionary expenses—must spend on this category)

- **Could Cut** (quasi-discretionary expenses—must spend on this category, but may be able to reduce the amount spent)

- **Cut!** (discretionary expenses—could completely eliminate spending in this category)

For example, you can't cut your mortgage or rent payment (at least not in the short-term). But you could probably cut back on what you spend on landscaping, and you can completely cut home improvements. (Be careful how much you cut from home repairs, however, since neglected repairs can lead to much bigger bills later.)

Go through your budget with the actual totals filled in and put a check mark in one of the three "Cut" boxes for each applicable budget item.

This will require some thought. For example, while you can't eliminate your real estate taxes completely, you might be able to get them reduced by filing an appeal regarding your assessment.

Or consider your telecommunications expenses. Many people are now "cutting the cord" and getting rid of their land-line telephone and that monthly bill. They rely solely on their cell phones. Speaking of which, have you checked to see if you are on the cell-phone plan that is the most economical for your style of use? Do you really need to be paying for all the non-voice features? Are you paying for the appropriate level of minutes for your needs?

And what about your cable/dish TV subscription? With all the other entertainment options available today—everything from Netflix to YouTube to blogging—do you even have enough hours in the day to take full advantage of the level of entertainment you're paying for? Can you save some money by reducing your level of service?

When you identify a reduction or complete cut you can make, strike through the amount in the Total column that represents what you're currently spending. Then pencil in the new, reduced amount next to it. For the budget items that you've decided to cut completely, strike through the Total for that item.

Electronic Bill Paying: Big Savings

 It's a shameless plug, but Fox Chase Bank (`www.foxchasebank.com`) offers free automatic electronic bill-paying. If you're not using free bill payment, you should take advantage of it. The savings can really add up.

Consider the out-of-pocket cost for paying a single bill by mail: 4 cents for the envelope, 1 cent for the check, and 44 cents (at this writing) adds up to about 50 cents per bill.

Assume 20 such bill payments a month, and you're at $10, month-after-month, for a total of $120 a year. Does this make sense, when you could pay those bills online for free? What would you do with an extra $120 a year? How about diverting it into a cash-reserve account?

Nothing Radical

Now that we're talking about cutting costs, it's very important to note that no one is calling for radical changes in your lifestyle. Reducing some expenses and completely eliminating others is not about submitting to a ration of bread and water.

All you have to do is find a way to reduce your expenses by 2% to 5% a month, and then divert that money into targeted savings and debt reduction. Just about anyone can do that.

And, now that you have a budget laid out, you have a much clearer idea of where those savings can come from.

Look at your discretionary spending categories and think about those things that you may be willing to give up in the short-term in order to get yourself into a better financial situation.

Take the cable TV bill for example: Maybe you're not ready to say goodbye to premium channels forever, but what impact could a temporary elimination of this bill have on your budget? What if you gave up this luxury for one year, and plowed all of those savings into reducing your credit-card debt?

You need to permanently change the way you think about money, and you need to concentrate on freeing up money on the margins. That's another way of saying that you've got to become conscious of your "unconscious" spending.

An "Unconscious Spending" Example

Several years ago, Kris was doing the bills, and it suddenly hit her. "Tom, do you have any idea how much money we're spending on dinners out each month?" Well, no, Tom didn't. It just happened.

We'd each get home from work, pretty much exhausted. Fixing dinner from scratch was just too much effort. Besides, didn't we deserve a little recreational dining for the day? Or we'd send out for a pizza or Chinese. Or we'd warm up some dish prepared and packaged by the local gourmet grocery store.

Adding it all up was an "OMG" moment for us. We are enthusiastic supporters of our local restaurants, but the dinner-out bills had gotten out of hand.

The main reason we ate out so frequently was that it was easier than cooking every night. Who wants to think about making dinner when you're tired from working all day?

So, we started planning ahead. Once or twice a week, Kris would make a casserole or a batch of soup, or a big order of grilled vegetables. We'd have those items in the refrigerator, ready to be heated when we got home from work.

We had a small chest freezer, and we'd make large portions of any recipe that could be frozen and store the remainders in the freezer for quick defrost and reheating. We also bought bulk packages of frozen fish and chicken on sale. We stored them in the freezer in individual portions. Preparing dinners became easy when there were numerous options available in the freezer or refrigerator. Pick a protein to grill or broil, add vegetables or a salad, and dinner is ready in a few minutes. Or simply reheat a casserole on really busy nights.

Occasionally, we would reward ourselves for our thrift by going to a nice restaurant on a Friday night.

This simple, pain-free approach (we both enjoy cooking together) cut our dining-out expenses considerably. And, yes, we channeled those savings into our several cash-reserve accounts.

Ta-Da! The Budget, Version 1

We were going to say that preparing a budget document is like kneading/needing bread dough. But we'll spare you the puns. The fact is that a budget really is a living document. The key point is that the budget says, "I have decided that I have this much money to spend and save each pay period, and I have decided where it will go."

So what do you do in the winter when your heating bills are particularly high? You shift budgeted funds from some other area, like entertainment, to cover the increased utility bills. In the spring and fall, when heating and cooling bills are basically nil, you might take that allocated money and splurge on food and drink to throw a party for your friends.

Changing How You Think About Money

This is the essence of what we mean when we say that you have to *change the way you think about money*. Money is not something you keep hitting the ATM for until it's all gone. Money is something you earn and then manage. And "managing" doesn't mean doing without, it means prudently shifting your expenditures month-to-month as the situation warrants.

Utility Budget Plans Can Help

Utility budget plans from oil, gas, and electric companies can help you level out the seasonal variations of heating and cooling bills and make it easier to stick to your budget.

Big car repair expense this month? Well, maybe you crank down the heat and pile on the blankets. Or deal with the heat with a powerful window fan instead of the AC. Maybe you brown-bag it to work for a couple of weeks and put off buying that new outfit you've been coveting—or wait until it goes on sale.

In any event, let's assume that you've penciled in some new numbers for your "Could Cut" and "Cut!" budget lines. Add them up and then compare the sum with your previous "What I'm spending now" sum.

Subtract.

So, what can you save? How much money?

Are you going to be in pain? Okay, go back and think about modifying some of the "Cut!" items. Maybe one dinner out per month instead of four or five, for example. Do a new total.

Where are you now?

The goal is to come up with a budget you can live with and really stick to. Remember, all you need is a 2% to 5% savings over what you're spending now.

Personal Allowances and Cash-Reserve Accounts: The Budget, Version 2

Line items for Personal Allowances and Cash-Reserve Account contributions have been part of the budget template from the start, but we are addressing them only now.

To reiterate: Giving yourself a personal allowance does two things. First, it frees you of the need to record and account for every little cash expense. And, second, it helps you control "unconscious" expenses.

You can spend your allowance on absolutely anything you want—gourmet coffee, a midday soda, a book or CD or DVD, snacks, and so on—but when the money's gone, it's gone. There's no hitting the ATM for more. Until your next payday.

As far as the cash-reserve accounts are concerned, you're going to have to decide what they are for. The goal is to set up and regularly fund accounts that will be available to pay for things you'd normally put on your credit cards. This is your bulwark against going deeper into debt. (A separate budget item is devoted to paying down the debt you're currently carrying.)

In the Introduction to this book, we suggested that cash-reserve accounts can be aimed at anything you like, including:

- Automobile Repairs and Inspections
- Clothing for Work
- Home Repairs and Appliances
- Vacations and Fun
- Tuition and Books

The goal is to build these funds up so that you never have to use your credit card to pay for these things. That's how you get off the credit-card-debt treadmill.

Once you've built robust cash-reserve accounts, you can start paying off your debt, starting with the card or loan carrying the highest interest rate.

Only You Can Decide

You'll have to decide for yourself how to focus your cash-reserve accounts and how much you will fund them each payday. Although we strongly suggest that you mark funding them as "Can't Cut" on your budget sheet. These should be "non-negotiable" expenditures.

And look, it's only $20 to $40 per account per paycheck. If you've been forthright about your budget, and the spending reductions you plan to make, it's hard to imagine that you can't find $100 (five cash-reserve accounts at $20 each per paycheck) to set aside.

It doesn't sound like much, but you'd be amazed at how it all adds up over time.

One final note: Once you finish your budget, bury your credit cards deep in a drawer! Make them hard to get at. You may need to leave just one of them in your wallet for emergencies, but make sure it's not the first thing you see when you open your wallet.

Principle 2:
Give Yourself an Allowance

Have you ever wondered why there are no windows in a casino? It's because casino owners know that you're likely to gamble longer if you don't know what time it is. In some establishments, dealers are even forbidden to wear watches.

When people are placed in a windowless room, they lose all track of time. Without a watch or the passing of the angle of the sun, our internal ability to keep track of time just does not exist. We have no built-in mechanism for doing it without external cues.

The same is true for our money. Without a budget, we simply don't have any idea where it goes. We don't have an internal apparatus for keeping track of money. It's not like food. Our stomachs will tell us when it's time to eat. But there's no similar organ that kicks in to tell us it's time to stop spending. Or that it's time to start saving.

Tom once asked a casino patron how he knew when to quit gambling. The guy said it was easy. He stopped when he was out of money.

Why an Allowance is the Answer

One of the secrets our advisor, Chris Oliver, taught us all those years ago was the importance of paying ourselves a weekly allowance. It sounds so obvious now, but it wasn't then. Chris asked us how we spent our money each week. We replied with an impressive list of things that included lunches, gas, car washes, and the like. But actually, we were improvising. We really had no idea where we were spending our cash.

Chris wasn't fooled. He asked us to write down every purchase for a week. We did, and we were amazed at the ways our money got spent. Most of it went for nonessential things that we gave little thought to buying and could not remember after the fact.

Kicking the ATM Habit

The truth is, it's simply too easy to spend money without much forethought if you can go to the ATM anytime you want. So Chris Oliver started both of us on a weekly allowance. We'll use Tom as an example of how this worked:

I would go the ATM once each week and withdraw $50. I could use that money any way I wanted. But I could only use the ATM once a week. I found that by putting myself on an allowance, I began to make better spending choices.

Do I really want to spend $4 on this, or do I want to save up to have a really nice lunch with the guys on Thursday? I began to make trade-offs, like taking my lunch to work some days so I had money to buy the latest CD I wanted. At first it was hard, but over time, I found that paying myself an allowance actually helped me to save more money, pay our credit cards off faster, and get to the financial freedom that we longed to achieve.

Even today, as the CEO of a bank, I still pay myself an allowance. It's a little bigger these days than it was back then. But the discipline still works.

Trade-offs and Choices

As we have said frequently in this book, to achieve financial freedom, you've got to change the way you think about money. And spending.

Suppose you've got $40 left of your cash allowance. You're thinking about going to see the latest blockbuster movie. In the past, you wouldn't have even considered the price. But by the time you've paid for your ticket, your "medium" popcorn, and your "small" soda, you'll be out close to $25. Which is fine. It's *your* allowance. You can spend it any way you want. That will leave you $15 for the rest of the week.

Cash to Call Your Own

Giving yourself an allowance of a set amount with no restrictions on what you can use it for is vital to sticking to your budget and to continuing your marital/relationship harmony.

Without some cash to call our own, we lose our sense of independence and personal freedom. And who among us hasn't on occasion said, "If I can't buy this thing that I want, what am I working for?"

As for relationships, both partners have to be on the same page for any budget to work. And that means that neither is dipping into the general fund for a night out with the guys (or gals) and other personal indulgences. That's what your allowance is for.

But, wait a minute. You also know that you're going out with your co-workers for beers on Thursday to celebrate a colleague's promotion. And you know it's never just one beer. It's going to be two, and then there are always munchies.

Bottom line: You're going to wind up having to put at least $15 down on the bar. That leaves you with nothing. But you know you're going to need at least $20 to get through the weekend.

So, what do you do? The "old" you would probably have both gone to the movie *and* the party, paying for the latter with a credit card (or another visit to the ATM). But the "new-and-improved" you stops to think about costs and available funds.

You make a conscious decision to go to the party and save the movie for next week, when you can pay for it out of that week's cash allowance. Or you can go to the movie, but forego the popcorn and soda. It's *your choice.*

"That's out of my price range. Do you have anything that's free?"

Goals vs. Commitment

Paying yourself a regular allowance is the beginning of your journey towards financial freedom, as Kris relates in this story:

> *When our friends Gwen and Steve first began to take control of their finances, it didn't take too long for Gwen to discover that her commitment was higher than Steve's. They had shared goals, but not shared commitment. Steve would frequently spend all of his allowance, and then go to the ATM for more cash. Gwen asked him to stick to the plan, but he couldn't help himself.*
>
> *This became a source of friction in their relationship. Eventually, Gwen solved the problem this way: she took Steve's ATM card and cut it in half. She started giving him his cash allowance every week. He wasn't very happy about that, but it was an important turning point for them. They did it that way for a year before Steve got*

another ATM card. After that year, our friends had achieved both shared commitment as well as shared goals.

How to Set Your Allowance

Under this system, you have two types of cash. One is what you can call your "weekly draw." This covers budgeted items like bus and train fare, turnpike or bridge tolls, and anything else you have identified as a budgeted expense.

The other type of cash is your allowance. This is for completely discretionary spending, like lunch or drinks after work, or books, movies, CDs and DVDs, morning coffee, newspapers, magazines, and just about any other cash purchase of about $20 or less. Basically, it's petty cash.

As Kris says:

I remember that I used to keep my draw money and my allowance money in separate parts of my wallet. I didn't want to spend any of "my" money on things that were part of our budget, like transportation to and from work.

Tom and I followed the same plan at home. We used to put cash for each expense into it's own labeled envelope. It's like a TV newsroom having a dozen clocks on the wall, each labeled with the name of a different city worldwide. No need to do the math. In an instant, you can see how much money you have on hand for each budgeted expense.

So, how do you decide what your allowance will be? A good way to start is to record where your petty cash goes for a week or two. As we found, doing this can be a huge revelation.

Identifying Needs vs. Wants

Once you've gathered your data, ask yourself which items you can reduce or eliminate. Try to draw a line between what you really need and what you just want.

For example, in this news-saturated era, do you really need to buy a daily newspaper? We have a friend who now reads the *Wall Street Journal* on his Kindle. By canceling his annual print subscription, he saved enough money to pay the full cost of that digital reader from Amazon.com. Owning a Kindle or one of its competitors can also cut costs for books, magazines, and lots of other publications for years to come.

And, as we said earlier, you may really need coffee on your commute, but you can brew your own instead of buying it at a convenience store.

Don't expect to get your allowance right on your first attempt. It may turn out that you can't comfortably do without certain things. So put them back in and cut or reduce something else. The goal is to become aware of your spending, to control your spending, and to avoid feeling so deprived that you stop holding yourself to your budget.

Brown Baggers of the World, Unite!

There are some "allowance" expenses you can't avoid, like going out with co-workers to mark some special event. Even though you might prefer to spend that money on something else, for good co-worker relations and office politics, you probably need to give in and celebrate with the gang. As long as those "special events" aren't happening every week!

Similarly, you don't have to go out to lunch at a restaurant with your co-workers every day. Some days, you can simply "brown bag it." Just as some people, for health reasons, choose a salad for lunch instead of a burger, you can say, "I'm brown bagging it for my financial health."

You'll find that when you're honest about your reasons for not going out, people will rally 'round and be supportive. They may even join you in forming a "Brown Baggers" group that only goes out for lunch once a month, or every other Friday.

Principle 3:
Restrict the Use of
Your Debit Card

Having established a budget and plugged the cash leak of "unconscious" spending with an allowance, the next logical step is to deal with that other leak, the debit card.

Let's not mince words. A debit card can be like a drug. We know this from personal experience. You carry it with you at all times, and whenever you see something you want, you hit the ATM to withdraw cash or you swipe the card at a store.

The problem is, of course, that the ATM has no boundaries. It only says "No" when your bank account is empty. Otherwise, it simply spits out whatever money you ask for.

The $38 Cup of Coffee

Actually, that's not completely true. Our industry—the banking industry—has discovered that the fees it can charge for overdraft protection" or "courtesy checking" can be hugely profitable.

Here's part of what Ron Lieber and Andrew Martin wrote on the subject in "The Card Game: Overspending on Debit Cards is a Boon for Banks" (*New York Times,* September 9, 2009):

> *When Peter Means returned to graduate school after a career as a civil servant, he turned to a debit card to help him spend his money more carefully.*

So he was stunned when his bank charged him seven $34 fees to cover seven purchases when there was not enough cash in his account, notifying him only afterward. He paid $4.14 for a coffee at Starbucks—and a $34 fee. He got the $6.50 student discount at the movie theater—but no discount on the $34 fee. He paid $6.76 at Lowe's for screws—and yet another $34 fee. All told, he owed $238 in extra charges for just a day's worth of activity....

Banks market it as overdraft protection, and the fees it generates have become an important source of income for the banking industry at a time of big losses in other operations. This year alone, banks are expected to bring in $27 billion by covering overdrafts on checking accounts, typically on debit card purchases or checks that exceed a customer's balance.

We know of banks that book over $1,000,000 a year—$25 at a time—on fees like this. Now, we're not going after the banking industry. Each institution has a fiscal responsibility to its shareholders. But we simply cannot accept this practice.

Speaking as bankers, we believe that our obligation is to help people with their money, not to profit from their poor financial-management skills. Our job is to help them manage better. And that's one of the main reasons we wrote this book.

Bank Overdraft Legislation Introduced

Bills have recently been introduced in both the U.S. House and Senate to regulate overdraft practices and fees. At this writing, there is no way to know what the final legislation will say. But indications are that consumers will be allowed to opt in or opt out of overdraft protection instead of being made part of such programs by default.

The practice by some banks of posting the largest transactions first, regardless of the sequence in which they occurred, may also be prohibited. This could actually work against consumers, because large transactions, like mortgage or car payments, might not clear because a lower-dollar-amount (less important) transaction cleared earlier in the day.

Should You Sign Up for Overdraft Protection?

 If you're in control of your accounts and in charge of your money, overdraft protection is a wonderful thing to have, just in case you forget about a check that you've written for a gift or for some other item that's not in your normal flow of things.

It can happen to anyone. Your mortgage check comes through for clearing. The last thing you want is for your bank to return the payment because you're $27 short in your account. The late fee on your mortgage payment is probably much more than $25. So you would much rather have the bank honor the check and charge you the $25 overdraft fee. If they bounce the check, you've got to call the bank to find out why. Then you'll have to call the mortgage company to explain. It has all the signs of a mini-nightmare.

Wants vs. Needs (Again)

The trick to using your debit card effectively is to use it only for things you really *need*. You need groceries, gasoline, and medicines. Those things really are needs. Everything else in your budget that you're going to spend cash on is a "want," not a "need." Now, of course, you have to be able to buy some "wants." You can't be so austere in your program that you deny yourself everything. So, leave yourself a few simple pleasures—but pay for them out of your personal allowance.

And another thing: Use your debit card to help you *keep track* of your budgeted expenses. Don't use it for non-budgeted expenses. By restricting your card's use to groceries, gasoline, and pharmacy expenses, you'll eliminate any doubts about whether you should use the card or pay cash for a given purchase.

As we've said before, even when you're considering buying something with cash, it's important to think about trade-offs and possibilities: "I could spend $30 for this bottle of wine or $15 for that bottle. Will my friends and I be able to taste the difference? And if I buy the less expensive bottle, I'll have 'saved' $15 that I could either put into one of my cash-reserve accounts or spend on something else that might give me more pleasure."

Remember: To achieve true financial freedom, you have to change the way you *think* about money and how you spend it.

Check the Web Before You Buy!

It's certainly not news to say that the Internet has changed everything. Everything, that is, but our old habits and ways of thinking about hunting for bargains. For example, consider the three types of purchases we suggest you use your debit card for:

Gasoline: It used to be that to find the best price on gasoline, you had to drive around town checking every gas station. And you always wondered whether this would cost you more in gas than you were likely to save. Today, you can simply go to Google and key in "gasoline prices" followed by your ZIP code. Or go to www.motortrend.com and enter your ZIP code there. This will produce a list of local stations and their current price per gallon.

Medicines: Finding the best price on your prescription drugs can be a bit more involved. Start by checking the Web site for your health insurance company. Most offer a searchable database of prescription drug prices, including brand-name and generic versions. (At this writing, both Walmart and Target offer a one-month's supply of many generic drugs for just $4.)

Groceries: The biggest savings can be had by using the Net to locate coupons and special offers on groceries. Check www.retailmenot.com for links to retail coupons of every sort. Also visit www.grocerysavingtips.com, where you'll find money-saving techniques for buying food, and links to leading supermarkets throughout the U.S. (Once you click through to a store in your area, you will often be able to print out individual coupons from that store's weekly circular.)

One final tip about grocery shopping: Don't shop hungry!

Principle 4:
Establish Cash-Reserve Accounts

This principle is at the heart of the process of achieving financial freedom. Establishing cash-reserve accounts for your major expected (and unexpected) expenses is the lever that will pry you free of your credit-card debt enslavement.

As we've said before, it's somewhat counter-intuitive. You would think that, having stopped the financial bleeding by creating a budget and staunching your cash outflow, the next step would be to start paying down your credit-card debt.

But here's the trick: As important as paying down debt is, what's even *more* important is avoiding taking on additional debt. That's what cash-reserve accounts are all about.

Wars are rarely won solely by single, decisive battles. They are won by planning, preparation, and patience. You may not be able to pay off your credit cards in one fell swoop. So you continue to pay the

"Remember, for the average American consumer, a credit-card purchase of $100 ends up costing $212. When you have cash-reserve accounts, that $100 expense will be only $100. That's a huge step forward!"—Tom Petro

monthly minimums, all the while building cash-reserve accounts to pay for the expenses you know are coming and for the unexpected expenses that inevitably crop up. This frees you from having to put new expenses on your credit cards.

A Tribute to Chris Oliver

It's important to acknowledge that we did not invent this system for achieving financial freedom all by ourselves. The seed was planted and germinated by our financial advisor, Chris Oliver. We adapted it for our own situation, of course, just as you should do.

The story begins when we were first married. We had very little financial help from our parents, who were occupied with helping our younger siblings through college. We set up housekeeping together and had no clue how to manage our money.

We both were making pretty good salaries. But no matter how much we earned, it never seemed to be enough. (Sounds familiar, doesn't it?)

We had no money saved. So naturally, we used credit cards and deferred-payment plans to get furniture for our apartment, to buy suits and clothing for work, to pay for car repairs, and to enjoy an occasional night on the town.

Unexpected Expenses?

Okay, maybe you didn't get the memo or the text message. So here it is again: There are always unexpected expenses. Always. No exceptions.

The car needs work for safety. The asphalt driveway needs to be sealed against the ravages of winter. The stove conks out. A pipe to the second-floor bathroom springs a pinhole leak, and your den ceiling starts to sag with the weight of the accumulated water.

Cue chorus: "Obla-dee, obla-da. Life goes on." If you happen to get through a month without an unexpected expense, consider it a gift.

It wasn't too long until we were swimming— actually "drowning"—in credit-card debt. We were making the minimum payments, but these seemed to only go up over time. The outstanding balances on our cards kept getting bigger and bigger.

Our credit scores were high, but so was our mounting debt. We felt trapped. We wanted to pay the cards off, but didn't have the money to do it.

Before long, we were complete slaves to our debt, spending more and more on interest payments every month, and less and less on the things that we wanted and that made us happy.

We made efforts to work down the level of debt on our cards, but we always met with frustration. It would seem like just as we were making progress, something unexpected would happen—a car would break down and need an expensive repair, the dryer would quit on us and have to be replaced. Tom's suit pants would fray and he'd have to buy a new suit.

Then we met Chris Oliver. Chris showed us a foolproof method for gaining control of our financial situation and getting out of the credit-card trap. He taught us to create cash-reserve accounts—and to stick a little money into each account with every paycheck.

Initially, our meager efforts to save didn't make much difference. But over time, we began to take charge of our finances. This was a revelation. And it is this method that we are so pleased to share with you.

Financial Freedom at Last!

Eventually, we had saved enough that when planned or unexpected things cropped up, we were able to draw on the funds set aside in our cash-reserve accounts and pay cash. That staved off accumulating any more credit-card debt.

And what about credit-card debt repayment? Well, once we got our cash-reserve accounts built up, we were able to begin targeting our cards and paying them down.

"THERE'S NOTHING WRONG WITH YOUR PERSONAL FINANCE SOFTWARE. YOU JUST DON'T HAVE ANY MONEY."

Now, here's the reality check: Getting out of debt took several years. (How could it be otherwise, unless you get an inheritance or some other windfall?)

Bottom line: By the time we were 30 years old, our only debts were our home mortgage and our car loan. Today, our only debts are mortgages for our two homes—one in Malvern, Pennsylvania, and one in Deer Valley, Utah. Everything else is paid for.

Ave Atque Vale

Chris Oliver died in November, 1989, from an aggressive form of cancer. He was not even 45 years old. We think about him often. We are grateful that he taught us the secret method of becoming debt free. We would not have discovered the secret—and been able to pass it along to you—without him.

What Accounts to Establish

Everyone's situation is different. The key take-away is the concept of creating cash-reserve accounts. Now, we realize that some people may find having seven or more separate accounts confusing. So, if you can accomplish the same thing with fewer accounts, by all means do so.

Nevertheless, there is something psychologically rewarding about having separate, freestanding accounts devoted to specific purposes. Among the accounts you might want to consider are the following:

- Automobile Maintenance and Inspections
- Home/Apartment Repairs and Appliances
- Clothing for Work
- Kids' School Clothing and Supplies
- Night School Tuition and Books
- Celebrations and Gifts
- Vacations and Fun

The **Automobile Maintenance and Inspections** account is for tires, brakes, oil changes, state inspection fees, and the like. We've spoken to automobile dealers and service-center operators, and they say that when the economy is bad, people tend to cut back on their regular maintenance.

That's understandable, but ultimately shortsighted. The money saved by putting off maintenance can cost you big-time further down the road, so to speak, when something serious goes wrong that could have been prevented had you not deferred maintenance and tended to the basics.

The **Home/Apartment Repairs and Appliances** account is for household items and repairs, like replacing the water heater or microwave oven. It's also for plumbers, electricians, and other service people you may need to call, or, as one of our older friends says, "When you need to get a man in."

The **Clothing for Work** and **Kids' School Clothing and Supplies** accounts are pretty self-explanatory. But what about **Night School Tuition and Books**? The notion here is that, while your employer may be paying for these things, they may not reimburse you until you have completed the course. So, you'll have to pay these expenses in the meantime.

"According to the Pew Research Center, one third of Americans say that unexpected expenses have seriously set them back. The most common cause is work-related—the loss of job or a cut in hours. Next is some sort of medical issue. A car problem is third. Expenses related to the home or housing are fourth. And life events or something going on in their children's lives is fifth."
—Kris Messner

What about **Celebrations and Gifts**? Many people don't budget for Christmas, Hanukah, or Kwanzaa gifts, but it's clearly a major expense item. The same is true of weddings, baby showers, bar/bat mitzvahs, graduations, and surprise birthday parties. After all, you don't know who in March of next year is going to send you, say, an announcement for a wedding in July. Your budget for this category will fluctuate based on where you are in the stages of life, but it just makes sense to set aside money for celebrations and gifts.

Vacations and Fun: A Very Special Account

We've saved the best for last: **Vacations and Fun**. You simply *have* to set up a cash-reserve account for this one. Thomas Jefferson once said, "I cannot live without books."

Were Jefferson alive today, he might have said, "I cannot live without my Kindle (or Sony) reader." Whatever. The point is that there are some things that we humans cannot live with out, and for us, vacations and fun are near the top of that list.

To put it another way, if you don't provide for vacations and fun, you'll never stick to the path that leads to financial freedom. So you should definitely put money aside for such things. But you should *think* about how you spend that money.

Hershey Park or the Franklin Institute?

For example, wouldn't it be great to take the family to Hershey Park! We love the town of Hershey, Pennsylvania, where the street lamps look like Hershey Kisses. But tickets for this little outing will cost you, at minimum, around $212 for a family of four. Plus gas, if you drive out from the Philadelphia area.

How about going to the Franklin Institute instead, for about $15 for adults and $12 for kids? For a family of four, call it $54, plus lunch or snacks. Throw in an IMAX theater experience for another $5 per person. That's still a savings of around $138.

Which will it be? We're not suggesting that the two experiences are equal. But that's not the point. The point is to have a nice day out with the family. And, once you pause to think about it, there are all kinds of ways to achieve that goal, without spending a lot of money or putting the outing on your credit card.

Funding Your Cash-Reserve Accounts

So how much should you put into your cash-reserve accounts each payday? Well, let's assume you're making $30,000 a year. That's a take-home pay of about $800 every two weeks. What if you could get to a 4% savings rate?

That would be $32 every paycheck. Assume that you've set up five cash-reserve accounts. That would mean that every two weeks, you would put $6.40 into each of your five accounts.

That may not sound like much, but if you are consistent and contribute each of the 26 times you get paid, over the course of the year, you'll have about $166 per account. For a total of $832. That's like getting an extra paycheck, and it's a super milestone.

Now suppose you could free up 8% for your cash-reserve accounts. That gives you $64 every paycheck. If you have five accounts, you're now talking about $12.80 for each one, every paycheck. If you do that over the course of a year, you're going to have about $333 in each account, for a total of about $1,665.

The key to this system, and why it's so beautiful, is that no matter how much you earn, even with very modest sums like this, you can stop being dependent on your credit cards and take charge of your financial life.

How Much is Enough?

Let's assume that you're several months or even a full year into this cash-reserve savings program. Your accounts are healthy. You're feeling more and more in control. When do you stop funding those accounts and switch over to paying down your credit cards and other debt?

A workable rule-of-thumb is this: Think about what might be your largest unanticipated expense. Then make sure you have enough in your cash-reserve account to cover it. And, of course, you can transfer money from one account to another.

So if your heater dies in mid-winter, and your Home Repair account doesn't have enough in it to cover the expense, "borrow from yourself" by taking money from your Celebrations and Gifts account. It's all your money.

Once again, it's important to emphasize that everyone's situation is different. Our point is to give you a system for regularly setting aside money, so you can avoid going into more credit-card debt. And so you can actively manage that money by anticipating and taking the time to think about the future.

Cash-Reserve Account Targets and Rewards

We can't tell you how much money you should have in each of your cash-reserve accounts. One approach is to set level targets for each one of, say, $400. If you have five accounts, that's $2,000.

Set a target timeframe as well. For example, "I would like to reach my $400 target for each account within 18 months."

Make your first goal to reach $100 in each account. Then celebrate this milestone. Treat yourself and your family to a movie or a night out at a nice restaurant. Do the same thing when you reach the next milestone of $200 in each account.

Granting yourself these small indulgences when you achieve milestones with your cash-reserve accounts is crucial to the success of this system.

When Using a Credit Card Can be a "Good Thing"

We're not against using credit cards. What we're against is carrying a credit-card balance. Paying with a credit card can have its advantages.

Let's say the guys delivering our new dishwasher manage to damage it getting it off the truck but install it anyway. If we've charged the dishwasher on a credit card, we can call the credit-card company and have them stop the transaction. That will get the appliance store's attention, and they will repair or replace the unit.

But if we've written a check for the dishwasher, we know that we're very likely to have a harder time. The store now has our cash, after all.

Similarly, there are the "points" and "rewards" one can earn by using a credit card. (We've read of parents charging a child's college tuition on a card for the free air miles they could earn.) There's nothing wrong with using the card for budgeted purchases, as long as you pay for them before the interest charges kick in.

What *is* wrong is using your credit card as an "extension" of your monthly income—to purchase non-budgeted items you cannot afford, and then not paying those items off every month. As we have said many times before, *think* before you purchase. Make your credit cards work for you. Get all the points and rewards you can, but pay your cards off every month using... wait for it... your cash-reserve accounts.

Now that we're in control of our finances, we use credit cards to our advantage. We've acquired television sets, airline tickets and free rental cars with our rewards points. But we always pay off our balance every month, because our purchases have been budgeted.

Your Rainy-Day Fund

You've established and funded your cash-reserve accounts. You've started paying down your credit cards and other debts. Skip ahead two or three years.

You've finally paid off all your debts. (Time for a "milestone" celebration!) Now you're ready for the next step.

"Wait a minute, what do you mean by 'next step'?"

We'll give it to you straight. On second thought, let's mix it up a bit: Suppose you lose your job. How are you going to pay the bills while you're looking for a new job? What if your spouse is the one who gets laid off? Will unemployment-benefit payments fill the income gap? And for how long?

Bottom line: What happens if your household income gets severely chopped? Bad things do indeed happen to good people. The only way to cope is to prepare. And that means creating a rainy-day account.

Fools and TV "Gurus"

We're going to have to hold ourselves back here. But the fact is, the advice you get from many financial "gurus" on TV couldn't be more wrong.

Consider: You're somebody taking home $800 every two weeks, $1,600 a month. When you just think about mortgage/rent payments, car payments, and everything else, that doesn't leave you with a whole lot of money to save or spend as you please.

Probably, you're earning $1,600 a month and spending $1,600 a month. You're living paycheck to paycheck, in other words. So listening to some TV money "guru" telling you that you should strive to have six times your monthly expenses in a savings account is ridiculous. That's $9,600! Are you kidding me?

Our solution is to lower the bar. Begin with the modest objective of saving one month's worth of expenses. When you achieve that goal, move on toward two months, then to three months' expenses. That's a quarter of a year. Keep going until you reach six months of expenses in reserve for a rainy day.

There's no question that having a rainy-day fund of six months' expenses is ideal. But is it doable? Yes, if you begin with modest milestones and work toward them over time. When you get your credit cards paid off, focus on a three-month goal. When you sock away one month's expenses, give yourself a milestone reward. Ditto for month number two. And so on.

Get Started Today!

When you set up cash-reserve accounts, you'll be taking a major step toward actively *managing* your finances. The more you practice these principles in your life, the more you'll begin to discover just how much freedom of choice you have as a result. You're actually gaining freedom and gaining control along the way, even while you still have some credit-card debt and other loans. So don't put it off. Get those accounts set up and start funding them today.

Fox Chase Bank Cash-Reserve Account Tools

 It's another shameless plug, but we cannot resist noting that Fox Chase Bank's Online Banking system allows you to set up multiple accounts at no cost. It's $25 to open a statement savings account, and once the account reaches $300, your money earns interest.

You can also give each account a nickname to identify the purpose for each account. And there are no monthly fees and no minimum-balance requirement for statement savings accounts. The bank's goal is to make it as easy as possible for you to set up multiple, named, cash-reserve accounts whenever you want.

Some employers will automatically direct funds into your different accounts, so be sure to check. If your employer doesn't offer this service, there's a simple solution. Using Fox Chase Bank's free online bill-paying service, you can actually set up your cash-reserve accounts as "bills" to be paid automatically.

Finally, you can arrange for the bank to notify you by secure cell-phone text message when certain events occur.

You'll find more information about these and other Fox Chase Bank account features in the Appendix section of this book.

Principle 5:
Start Paying Off
Your Debts

Net worth equals your assets (what you have) minus your liabilities (what you owe), and there are only two ways to increase net worth. One way is to increase your assets. The other is to reduce your debts.

Assets are subject to value fluctuations. Stocks go up and down. The value of your home will go up and down. But if you pay off your debt, you get a *guaranteed* return on your investment. Nothing else is more powerful.

For example, if you're being charged 19% interest on your credit card, paying off your balance will generate an automatic 19% return to you. There's no risk, no fluctuation in value, no depreciation, and the return is immediate.

That's why it makes so much sense to reduce your liabilities before trying to increase your assets.

Earlier, we looked at the power of compound interest. Well, that power cuts both ways. When it's applied to assets, it's your friend. But when it's applied to your debts, it's your foe.

Mortgage Magic

Consider this: Let's say George borrowed $250,000 for his home. He got a 30-year fixed-rate loan at 5%. His monthly payment is $1,342.05 (excluding escrow for insurance and taxes). His total payments over 30 years will be $483,138. That's almost *twice* what George originally borrowed.

Now, here's a bit of "magic." George can pay off his mortgage nine years early by adding an additional $250 per month toward his payment. If he did that, the lifetime cost of his mortgage loan would drop to $401,000, for an astonishing savings of $82,000.

How Credit-Card Companies Calculate Minimum Payments

 Just like a mortgage payment, your credit-card payment includes a principal payment plus an interest payment. The minimum principal payment is different for every credit-card issuer (it will be disclosed in the terms and conditions for your account), but it generally ranges from 2% to 4% of the outstanding balance.

Let's assume an outstanding balance of $8,000, a 2% minimum principal payment, and an interest rate of 19%.

1. Begin by calculating the minimum principal payment using this formula:

    Balance x Minimum Payment Percentage = Principal Due

    $$\$8,000.00 \times 0.02 = \$160.00$$

2. Next determine the amount of interest due for the month. Begin by adjusting your interest rate so you can calculate one month's interest and multiply that by your outstanding balance:

    Interest Percentage/12 x Balance = Interest Due

    $$0.19/12 = 0.016 \times \$8,000.00 = \$126.67$$

3. Finally add the minimum principal payment and the interest amount to get the total minimum monthly payment::

    Principal Due + Interest Due = Minimum Payment Due

    $$\$160.00 + \$126.67 = \$286.67$$

Pay More Than the Credit-Card Minimum

The same "mortgage magic" applies to credit cards. On the opposite page, we lay out how credit-card companies calculate the minimum payment due each month. As you will see, if you owe $8,000 on a card with an annual percentage rate (APR) of 19%, your minimum payment will be $286.67.

If you're among the 42% of Americans who pay only the minimum on your credit cards, even if you never use a given card again, it will take you *more than 20 years* to pay off a credit-card debt of $8,000. Over that time, you will not only pay back the $8,000, you will also pay $26,896 in interest.

Minimum Payment Calculators

If you'd like to check your own payoff time horizon, go to www.creditcards.com/calculators, click on "Minimum Payment Calculator," and enter the simple information it requests.

Or do a Google search on "credit card minimum payment calculator." There are lots of them out there.

When you're building up your cash-reserve accounts, you may have no choice but to pay only the minimums on your credit cards. But paying only the minimums is clearly not a good long-term approach.

Once you get your cash-reserve accounts built up, focus on your highest rate card and make every effort to pay double, triple, or even quadruple the minimum, while you continue to pay the minimums on your other cards.

And, as you know by now, we're very big on rewards. So when you get that first card paid off, celebrate. (Just don't use a credit card to do it.) Then it's on to the card with the next highest annual percentage rate.

Don't Cancel Your Cards!

It is the most natural, seemingly common-sense action in the world: I've paid off that card, now I'm going to cancel it. But we are here to tell you: Don't do it! Cut it up. Hide it away. But don't cancel the account.

Actually, let's modify that. If you have 10 cards, you should definitely cancel some of them. The ones with the shortest credit history should be candidates for cancellation. Hold on to the ones with the longest credit history.

Indeed, be aware that canceling a credit-card account can actually hurt your credit score. (We'll have more to say about credit scores in a moment.)

In our globalized, move-at-the-speed-of-light economy, credit scores offer lenders a quick, single-number solution to determining if you're credit-worthy and if so, how high to set your credit-card/borrowing limits. Increasingly, credit scores are also used to check you out before you can rent an apartment or before an employer will hire you.

Back in the '60s

To put this into perspective, we have an older friend who used to sell photocopiers for a living. It was the 1960s, and whenever Bob needed to borrow $500 for a home-improvement project, he would don his "banker's suit" and go into town to meet with a vice president of the local bank.

The bank VP would go over Bob's financials—the value of his home, the total of what he owed, and the total of what he earned, and so on. (Credit cards were not a major factor until the mid-to-late 1960s.) As far as we know, Bob always got the loan. But this kind of personal, face-to-face interaction was how loans were made back then.

Today, every lender we can think of relies primarily on an individual's credit report and credit score. So you won't need your "banker's suit," but you will need a good report and score.

Credit Reports, Scores, and Repayment History

The reason not to cancel all of your paid-off credit cards is that the companies that calculate your credit score pay particular attention to your repayment history. This makes a lot of sense for at least two reasons.

Credit Reports vs. Scores

Your *credit report* is a record of your borrowing and repayment history, including late payments and bankruptcies. Your *credit score* is a single number based on a statistical analysis of your credit report.

First, lenders who approve credit limits and loans are dealing with a universe of some 190 million or more potential customers.

Second, credit-card "loans" are what we bankers refer to as "unsecured debt." A car loan is secured by the car. A home mortgage is secured by the land and the house. All of which means that should the borrower default on the loan, the lender can sell the car or the property to recoup its losses.

The money bankers allow credit-card users to borrow is secured by... nothing. All they have to go on is the history you have built up demonstrating that you are a reliable re-payer. And your excellent repayment history is what you lose if you cancel a card that you have paid down to zero.

Pay as Much as You Can in Cash

Here's an interesting and all too-common situation. Your clothes-dryer dies. A new one will cost $500, delivered and installed. But all you've got in your household cash-reserve account at the time is $300.

Cash is King

Many people are not aware that most merchants would far rather accept cash than credit cards. That's because credit-card companies charge merchants a fee for every transaction. Offer to pay with cash, and ask the merchant for a cash discount.

The answer? Do one of two things. Ask the merchant if he or she will accept $300 in cash and $200 charged to your credit card. This should not be a problem in the majority of cases.

If it turns out to be a problem, put the entire purchase on your credit card and send a check for $300 to the credit-card company. Do it immediately, and you won't incur any finance charges on that transaction.

You can do this? Of course you can! This is just another part of altering how you think about money and debt repayment.

There are good reasons to charge certain expenses. The dryer example just cited is a great case in point. Suppose the dryer was damaged en route to your home or apartment. If you had paid cash, you would be forced to wrangle with the store to fix or replace it. But if you had charged it, you could file a dispute with the credit-card company and get them to intervene on your behalf.

We're not saying you should never use your credit cards, but responsible use of credit cards means that purchases are budgeted and paid for without interest charges.

What You Need to Know About Credit Reports

Credit is established by building a history of borrowing and timely debt repayment. That's why, if you are just starting life as an adult, the best thing you can do is to borrow some money and pay it back on time.

Doing so will give you a credit record, and a favorable one at that. You can be the richest person on earth, but if you don't have a credit record of some sort, you probably will be turned down for a loan. That's simply the way the system works.

Credit Bureaus

There are three leading credit bureaus:

- **Equifax** (www.equifax.com)

- **Experian** (www.experian.com)

- **TransUnion** (www.transunion.com)

These companies create and maintain files on the credit histories of the millions of people in the United States who have a department store charge account, a car loan, a student loan, a home mortgage, or Visa, MasterCard, and other credit cards. They also incorporate information drawn from public records, such as bankruptcies, foreclosures, tax liens, and court judgments.

Credit bureaus also collect a constant stream of current information supplied by retailers, credit-card companies, and others regarding your payment history. If you are a week late paying your mortgage in January due to holiday bills, that fact (though not the reason you were late) will be reported and recorded. It will become part of your credit report.

Credit reports are the reason why you want to make sure you're paying at least the minimum on each of your credit cards. If you don't, you'll show up as "delinquent." And that's the last thing you want.

Late Payments

We would never encourage anyone to be late or to skip a payment. At the same time, it's important to point out that what lenders are looking for in credit reports are *patterns* of repayment behavior.

They want to see your overall repayment trend, in other words. Unless a huge amount of money is involved, a blip here and there is not usually significant.

Controlling the How Much Credit They Give You

Kris has a great story to tell about *not* having any credit-card balances:

We recently refinanced our home here in Malvern. That involved the lender pulling our credit report, which was fine, but we seemed to have a negative. Namely, we didn't have any outstanding credit-card balances.

Since we pay off our credit cards monthly, we haven't had a credit-card balance in years. Why isn't that a positive instead of a negative? The answer is that credit-rating agencies want to see an indication that you have a history of regularly repaying what you owe. They also want to know how much credit you have access to.

As bankers, we understand the game better than most. We just choose not to play it. Except, sometimes you must. So when we had to buy a new freezer, I went to Sears and said, "Alright, I need a new credit card so I can charge this freezer." We could have paid cash for it, but I wanted to establish at least one revolving-credit account. They gave me a limit of $5,000.

Knowing about credit-rating agencies, I said, "I don't want $5,000. I only want $2,000." They were fine with that. But I know they were surprised, since most customers apparently request more credit than they are given.

Getting a Copy of Your Credit Report

You should know that by law, you have the right to get a free copy of your credit report once every 12 months. The place to go is www.annualcreditreport.com. This site is owned and operated by the three leading credit-reporting agencies.

You also have the right to provide credit bureaus with a 100-word statement explaining the circumstances related to specific information in your report.

Examples might include late payments due to an illness, a divorce-related problem, or a dispute with a manufacturer. Credit-reporting companies are required by law to include such statements in your credit report.

If you find inaccuracies in your reports, the law requires that they be corrected within 30 days after you notify the credit bureau of the mistakes.

Impact of Credit Reports and Scores on Interest Rates

The interest rate you are charged when you borrow money is directly related to your credit report and score. We've all heard TV ads for car loans at low rates for "qualified buyers." Whether or not you're "qualified" depends on your credit score.

If you have a great score, you might be charged 1.9%. If your score is not so great, you might be charged 10%, 12%, or 15%.

And, once notified of an error, the bank or other business that supplied the incorrect information is required to correct its records so that the same error doesn't keep appearing on your credit report.

For more information on credit reports and your rights under the law, visit www.ftc.gov/credit.

Credit Scores: The Crucial Element

As we said earlier, credit scores and credit reports are two different things, even though they are closely related.

Credit scoring started in 1956 when engineer Bill Fair and mathematician Earl Isaac, two former Stanford Research Institute researchers, got excited by the newly emerging computer technology. They wanted to find ways to help companies apply it to their business challenges.

A Warning About
"Imposter" Credit Report Web Sites

The following warning can be found on the Federal Trade Commission Web site:

> Only one website is authorized to fill orders for the free annual credit report you are entitled to under law — annualcreditreport.com. Other websites that claim to offer "free credit reports," "free credit scores," or "free credit monitoring" are not part of the legally mandated free annual credit report program. In some cases, the "free" product comes with strings attached. For example, some sites sign you up for a supposedly "free" service that converts to one you have to pay for after a trial period. If you don't cancel during the trial period, you may be unwittingly agreeing to let the company start charging fees to your credit card.

> Some "imposter" sites use terms like "free report" in their names; others have URLs that purposely misspell annualcreditreport.com in the hope that you will mistype the name of the official site. Some of these "imposter" sites direct you to other sites that try to sell you something or collect your personal information.

> Annualcreditreport.com and the nationwide consumer reporting companies will not send you an email asking for your personal information. If you get an email, see a pop-up ad, or get a phone call from someone claiming to be from annualcreditreport.com or any of the three nationwide consumer reporting companies, do not reply or click on any link in the message. It's probably a scam. Forward any such email to the FTC at spam@uce.gov.

They created Fair Isaac Company, which later changed its name to FICO. (Check www.myfico.com for consumer-friendly information on what the company provides.) The company's main product is the FICO credit score.

Each of the three leading credit bureaus has a similar scoring system, but FICO is the most widely used. Credit scores strive to summarize a person's credit worthiness in a single three-digit number.

Five Factors Go Into Your Credit Score

FICO scores range from 300 to 850. Generally, a score under 650 means that you are considered a higher risk. Below 500 and you will likely not qualify for any bank loans at all, and you'll be forced to work with a payday lender or pawn shop.

A score above 700 means you're a good credit risk. A score above 775 means you have the highest caliber credit. Only information contained in your credit report is used to determine your FICO score. The higher the score, the more credit-worthy you're considered to be.

Here are the five factors that determine your score:

1. **Payment History**. Your history of paying your loans, revolving credit, and credit cards on time accounts for 35% of the score. Late payments will lower your score, so it's best to pay on time. Adverse actions recorded in public records will also lower your score. These include bankruptcy, liens, judgments, wage attachments, and uncollected amounts that have been charged off.

2. **Amounts Owed**. The amounts you owe account for 30% of your score. This includes the proportion of original loan amounts still owed by you, as well as the percentage of credit lines and credit-card available balances that are in use. Generally, the lower the percent of available credit that you owe, the better. Surprisingly, having no revolving credit or active credit cards will actually hurt your score.

3. **Credit History**. The length of your credit history accounts for 15% of your score. This includes how long each account has been open and how long it has been since each account was last used. Generally, active use of credit with a history of paying on time will drive a better score. Paying

your credit cards in full every month does *not* lower your score.

4. **New Credit**. New credit accounts for 10% of your score. This includes credit inquiries as well. Too many credit inquiries (from potential employers, landlords, car dealers, etc.) will lower your score.

5. **Type of Credit**. The type of credit you use accounts for 10% of your score. Lenders look for an indication that you know how to handle money. So you get higher marks if you have a mortgage, car loan, and credit-card balances than you would if you only have credit-card balances.

FICO vs. Other Sources of Credit Scores

The law does not require any company to give you your credit score for free. And, as we've said, FICO credit scores are based on credit-bureau reports, which can vary, as explained in this excerpt from the myFico.com site:

> *Your FICO scores often vary from bureau to bureau—this fluctuation could be the difference between a low interest rate and a high one. Differences may be caused by errors in one or more of your credit reports; errors you may be able to correct.*
>
> *If you're planning a major purchase, like a home or car, it's a good practice to check both of your scores and negotiate the best rate. For example, a 50-point score variance could cost you more than $200/month in mortgage payments.*

Now, it's important to note that the myFICO site will sell you your credit-bureau-specific FICO score for $15.95 each. So the company is clearly interested in getting you to pay for this information. And probably you should.

Other sites will sell you your credit score for about half the price, but the score you get may be a "consumer" version of your FICO score. Only myFICO.com and Equifax.com sell actual FICO scores to consumers.

"We've got borrower's remorse."

Credit-Counseling Services

We'll wrap up this chapter with a few words about credit-counseling services. If you find yourself really in over your head with credit-card and other types of debt, look for a nonprofit organization that offers counseling services.

A good place to start is the Consumer Credit Counseling Service of Delaware Valley (800-989-2227, www.cccsdv.org). Since 1966, this outstanding not-for-profit organization has helped more than 500,000 people gain control of their finances and improve their lives though one-on-one credit counseling and financial education. These efforts have in turn, supported neighborhood stability and improved the quality of life for individuals and families in the Philadelphia region.

We strongly advise *against* contacting an attorney or firm that promises to consolidate your debts in return for a percentage of what you owe. Such companies typically list themselves under "Credit and Debt Counseling Services" in the Yellow Pages. Stay away from them.

Seven Ways to Improve Your Credit Score

1. Pay your bills on time. If you have a spotty record, get caught up and then stay current.

2. Keep your credit-card balances low compared to the credit you have available. Try to keep your outstanding balance below 25% of what you can borrow.

3. Keep your accounts open longer. Many people will close one card and transfer the balance to a new card every time they get a better deal. Frequent switching—opening a new account and closing the old one—will tend to lower your credit score.

4. Minimize new credit requests. Every time a lender asks for a copy of your credit report, that inquiry is recorded. If you know that you will be applying for a new car loan or borrowing to buy or refinance a house, don't apply for new credit cards beforehand.

5. Pay your credit cards and retail finance loans on time. Timely payment on all your loans matters, but these revolving-credit accounts carry more weight. Make sure that your payments aren't late. Also, pay your utilities on time every month.

6. Resolve disputes with creditors. If you have a billing problem, don't ignore it. Any professional or business that you owe can turn your account over for collection and the disputed amount can become a problem on your credit report.

7. Finally, remember that credit scores change over time. If you have a blemish on your credit report, you can improve your score by making sure that you stay current on all your loans and credit cards.

Principle 6:
Pay Yourself First

Paying yourself first is all about retirement. Yes, it is absolutely vital to fund your cash-reserve accounts and to start paying down debt. But it is equally important to begin building your retirement savings as soon as possible. Because of the power of compound interest, delaying by even a year or two can cost you big-time years hence.

There are two things we can say about retirement. First, it can be hard to discipline yourself to save for a need that's probably a

> *"The one thing you can be sure of is that however much you think you're going to need for retirement, it probably isn't enough."* —Kris Messner

long way in the future. Second, it's tough to know "how much is enough." The one thing you can be sure of is that however much you think you're going to need for retirement, it probably isn't enough.

As we said earlier in the book, the general rule of thumb is that you'll need between 70% and 100% of your former salary to continue to live in retirement the same way you lived when you were working. Yes, some costs, like commuting and work clothing expenses, go away when you retire. But others, like travel, hobbies, and doctor visits may take their place.

If Social Security continues to function the way it has in the past, it will probably cover only about 40% of your needed income. Where's the other 60% going to come from?

"If we take a late retirement and an early death, we'll just squeak by."

Calculating What You'll Need

L et's put some actual numbers with these facts. Suppose your final salary is $50,000 before taxes. To keep it simple, just assume that's the amount you'll need each year for a comfortable retirement. If your Social Security income covers about 40% ($20,000), your retirement savings will have to generate $30,000 a year.

And how much will you need in retirement savings in order to do that? One way to figure it is to use the "Rule of 25." According to Walter Updegrave, *Money Magazine* senior editor, "You can estimate the size of the nest egg you'll need by multiplying the annual income you want in retirement by 25."

Applying the Rule of 25 to our example, to generate $30,000 from savings in retirement, you'll need to build a nest egg of roughly $750,000. This assumes that you'll be getting Social Security, and that you'll be withdrawing 4% of your nest egg each year when you retire. It does *not* account for inflation. So the actual dollar amount you'll need will be higher than it would be in today's money. (At an average inflation rate of 3% a year, your cost of living doubles every 24 years.)

These are rough, back-of-the-envelope figures, but even a more precise calculation would yield a result of the same magnitude. Seven hundred fifty thousand dollars!

And yet, according to the Retirement Confidence Survey conducted in 2009 by the Employee Benefit

How Much Will You Get from Social Security?

The Social Security Administration has a very impressive Web site at www.socialsecurity.gov. Among many other things, you can request a copy of your annual Social Security Earnings Statement, and you can use the site's calculator to estimate the benefits you will receive when you retire. (It's a secure site, so don't be concerned about entering your Social Security number.)

Research Institute, "Fifty-three percent of workers report less than $25,000 in total savings and investments (excluding their home and defined-benefit plans)." The workers surveyed were between 25 and 55+ years old. (For more details, go to the EBRI Web site at www.ebri.org.)

What Are Your Options?

When you focus your mind on saving and planning for retirement, you will discover that you have many options. In this section we're going to introduce you to three of the "biggies":

- 401(k) Plans
- Individual Retirement Accounts (IRAs)
- Roth IRAs

They're all good deals that, frankly, you'd be foolish not to investigate. But the truth is that there are so many retirement savings options and plans open to most people that we strongly encourage you to seek professional advice.

Your 401(k) and the Power of the Match

Whether the amount of savings you need is $750,000 or $1,000,000 or more, just the thought of getting there is daunting. But there are powerful forces on your side. Most people are just not aware of them.

One such force is time and "the miracle of compound interest." Another is tax-deferred savings. Still another is employer matching.

Let's look at the last one first. If you work for a company, there's a good chance that it offers its employees the option of participating in a 401(k) or 403(b) plan. Both are named for the sections of the U.S. tax code that put them into force (Section 401, paragraph k, for example). A 403(b) plan is basically a 401(k) for non-profits and state or municipal workers.

When you enroll in your company's 401(k) plan, a certain percentage of your pre-tax income each pay period is put into an account, and some percentage of that contribution is often matched by your employer.

Here's an example:

Mary starts saving $50 per pay in her Fox Chase Bank 401(k) plan on her 30th birthday. Her 401(k) investments earn 8% a year. Fox Chase Bank matches Mary's contributions 33.3% with every pay, or $16.67. As a result, when Mary retires at age 65, she will have $305,843 in her retirement plan.

Over the course of her career, Mary will have made total payments of $45,500 to her 401(k) account ($50 per pay × 26 pay periods per year × 35 years). Fox Chase Bank will have matched her *contributions by contributing $15,152 (33.3% times $50 = $16.67 per pay x 26 pay periods x 35 years).*

Compounding did the rest of the work, converting $60,652 of paid-in savings (Mary's elective deferral plus the bank's match) into $305,843. That's the power of the match, the power of time, and the power of saving money on a tax-deferred basis.

Mary will have to pay tax when she starts to withdraw from the account, but the tax rate will almost certainly be lower than when she was working. And, by the way, by contributing pre-tax income, Mary reduces the amount upon which the IRS figures her tax, so she'll owe less income tax each year she's working.

There are just two main catches. First, there are limits on the dollar amount you can contribute each year. And once you start contributing to a plan, you can't touch the money until you're 59.5 years old. (There are exceptions, but they involve paying income tax *plus* a 10% penalty.)

The bottom line is this: If your employer offers a 401(k) plan, sign up for it and contribute at least enough to take full advantage of the employer matching funds.

Individual Retirement Accounts

Entire books have been written on planning and saving for retirement. Our goal here is to raise your awareness of the need to start saving as soon as possible, and to alert you to some of the leading "financial instruments" available to you.

Everyone's situation is different, and ideally, your company will have a benefits counselor you can consult. Still, one important option to consider, whether or not you have access to a 401(k), is an Individual Retirement Account (IRA). This account has nothing to do with your employer. You have to take the initiative and set it up yourself.

You also have to make the contributions yourself—up to the maximum allowed per year. In 2009, the maximum contribution was $5,000 if you're 49 or younger, $6,000 if you're 50 or older. The contribution limit increases each year in increments of $500, depending on the level of inflation.

So, where's the benefit? The benefit is that you can take whatever you contribute to your IRA as a tax deduction. That reduces your taxable income and means you're funding the account with pre-tax dollars. You also have considerable flexibility in where you invest those funds.

The lesson is this: First, fund your 401(k) to the fullest extent possible so that you maximize your employer's match. Second, set up an IRA and fund it to the max as well. (If you're self-employed, look into a Keogh and a Simplified Employee Pension Plan IRA.) Third... well, there's this very intriguing option called a Roth IRA, which is what we'll discuss next.

Roth IRAs

Named for Delaware Senator William Roth, who sponsored the legislation in 1997, a Roth IRA is an IRA funded with after-tax dollars. In other words, in contrast to a traditional IRA, you don't get any deductions for the amount you contribute to a Roth IRA.

"Why would I want to do that?" you ask. Well, because you have already paid tax on the money you contribute, you're allowed to withdraw those contributions at any time, tax-free. In addition, your Roth IRA contributions grow tax-free over time. And when you turn 59.5 years old, you can withdraw all the money in the account tax-free.

That's right: No taxes on all of the capital gains, interest, dividends, etc., that your fund has earned over the years. It's almost like "free money." Well, "tax-free," at least.

Of course, there are limitations. The maximums you can contribute are identical to the maximums that apply to traditional IRAs as discussed above. But there are income cutoffs.

For example, in 2009 you could contribute the maximum as long as your income was below $105,000 as a single income-tax filer, or below $166,000 if you file a joint return.

Get Professional Retirement Planning Advice

Sometimes it seems that Congress spends more time fiddling with tax laws than it does campaigning for re-election. The result is that retirement savings plans—*your* retirement savings plans—can be a moving target. The laws change. The requirements and limitations change. It's really too much for the average person who's just trying to scratch out a living to handle on his or her own.

You should get professional advice. Look for someone who charges a flat fee or hourly rate, rather than billing on a commission basis. Many people who style themselves as "financial planners" are really in the business of selling you insurance policies.

That's not necessarily a bad thing. But you might be better off in the end seeking out a CPA (Certified Public Accountant) who will work with you on an hourly or fixed-fee basis.

Is it worth paying an experienced professional several hundred dollars to help you set up the accounts and plans you need to save for a comfortable retirement? Think of it this way: If you sleep 8 hours a day, you spend one third of your life on a mattress. So what would you pay for that mattress?

If you retire at 65 and live to 85, you'll be spending nearly a quarter of your life retired. So what would you pay to have a professional help you take the steps you need to take today to make sure that your retirement is comfortable with no money worries?

The Early-Saver's Advantage

We hope that what we've said so far has gotten you thinking about the specific steps you need to take to insure a comfortable retirement—however many years in the future that may be. Now we'd like to pull back and direct your attention to the big picture.

Namely, the incredible power of *time* when it comes to building wealth. The numbers don't lie. There are no questionable assumptions.

These are the facts:

> If you were to begin at age 25 depositing 10% of your salary—let's call it $3,000 a year—into a tax-deferred account, in 15 years when you turn 40, you would have close to $84,000, assuming an interest rate of 7% percent. If you then *stopped* contributing but let your investment continue to grow, by the time you turned 65, you would have almost $456,000. (And keep in mind that what you paid in was $45,000—$3,000 for 15 years.)

Change the assumed interest rate and the results will change. But know this: Historically, an investment in a no-load (no-fee) stock market index fund has grown at a rate of around 9% to 10% a year. So our 7% assumption is conservative if you have a long time window.

Think about that: You pay in $45,000 and you end up with more than ten times as much: $456,000! And think about what you'd have if, instead of stopping at age 40, you continued saving $3,000 a year until you retired at 65 (25 more years). And don't forget that as your salary rises over time, that $3,000 will become a lower and lower percentage of your income.

So, can you reach the previously mentioned target of saving $750,000 or more in your retirement fund? Sure you can. If you start early. Never, ever, ever underestimate the power of compounding interest over time. If you start late, you can still do it. You'll just have to put in more money—a larger percentage of your paycheck—to catch up.

First Things First: Your Cash Cushion

As important as it is to begin saving for retirement as soon as possible, building a cash cushion or rainy-day fund is even more important. This will be money you've saved against getting laid off or having unexpected expenses. As we've said before, save enough to cover your living costs for at least three months.

Build your cash-reserve accounts so you can stop using credit cards. Then add the rainy-day fund to your budget and start building it as well. When you have enough in the rainy-day fund to cover three months of expenses, start paying down your credit cards. The three-month mark is also the time to begin saving for retirement.

Note the difference between cash-reserve accounts, your rainy-day fund, and your retirement savings:

- **Cash-reserve accounts** are part of your budget. They contain money you intend to spend.

- The **rainy-day fund** is for life emergencies. The money it contains should be reachable. That is, it should be in an account where you can lay your hands on it quickly without paying penalties or withdrawal charges.

- Your **retirement fund** is a long-term investment. In general, the longer you're willing to tie up your money, the higher the rate it will earn.

Invest Rainy-Day Savings in a CD Ladder

B ecause your rainy-day fund is designated for periods of disruption in your life, you probably won't need to access it all at once. It has to be available to you in the event of a financial emergency, but you'd also like it to earn good returns.

You'll want to keep this in bank savings rather than in stocks, bonds, or mutual funds. Why? Let's say you get laid off from work. Your company has to downsize because sales have gone through the floor. The economy is probably bad—maybe even in a recession.

Guess what? The stock market is probably down too. Just when you need your rainy-day funds the most, they have lost 20%, 30%, or even 50% of their value. That's why we urge you to keep your rainy-day funds in safe FDIC-insured savings accounts.

The highest liquidity—the ease with which you can get your hands on the money—and the best returns come together in a certificate of deposit (CD).

You'll never lose your principal with a CD, but if you have to tap it before its maturity date, you'll forfeit any interest that principal has earned. So it just makes sense not to put all of your funds into a single CD basket.

The Benefits of CD Laddering

That's what makes "CD laddering" so appealing. This technique allows you to take advantage of interest rates spread over a range of maturities without sacrificing liquidity. The trick is to invest in several CDs with staggered maturity dates. Remember: The longer you're willing to tie up your money, the higher rate it earns.

A ladder can be as long or as short as you like, but for this example let's use a five-year ladder with five rungs.

If you have $10,000 to invest, you could put all of it into a single certificate of deposit like a two-year CD. But what would happen if you needed all or part of that money before the CD matured? You would have to take an early withdrawal. You'd get the $10,000 back, but you would forfeit the accumulated interest. A better way is to create a CD ladder.

> *"A CD ladder eliminates the emotional decision-making associated with an investment or savings plan. It evens out the highs and lows that invariably come with interest-rate cycles, while providing flexibility in the event that you need to access your rainy-day funds."* —Tom Petro

Here's an example:

Rung #	Type of CD	Time to Maturity	Amount	Interest Rate
Rung 1	1-year CD	1 year	$2,000	1.50%
Rung 2	2-year CD	2 years	$2,000	1.80%
Rung 3	3-year CD	3 years	$2,000	2.45%
Rung 4	4-year CD	4 years	$2,000	2.95%
Rung 5	5-year CD	5 years	$2,000	3.35%
Total Investment and Average Return			**$10,000**	**2.41%**

After a year, the one-year CD occupying the first rung matures and each of the other CDs moves down a year. In other words, the two-year CD now matures in one year; the three-year is two years from maturity, etc. The money from the one-year CD that has just matured is rolled over into the now vacant five-year rung. Every year you're replacing the rung that's farthest out—in this case the five-year rung.

The ladder creates a natural process where you always replace the longest maturity—the top rung on the ladder—so you always reap the benefit of getting the highest rates. Also, by having a ladder, you're only re-investing a portion of your money when yields are low.

Finally, the ladder provides flexibility. If you needed to take an early withdrawal for a financial emergency, you would only forfeit interest on one $2,000 CD.

Credit-Union Deposits Are *Not* FDIC-Insured

Did you know that credit-union deposit accounts are not FDIC-insured? It's true. If you want FDIC insurance, you must have your deposit account with a bank or savings and loan.

The basic FDIC insurance amount is $250,000 per depositor, per insured bank. Deposits maintained in different categories of legal ownership at the same bank can be separately insured. Therefore, it's possible to have deposits of more than $250,000 at one insured bank and still be fully insured.

What to Do with a Windfall

In the Middle Ages, kings, princes, barons, and the like were very possessive about what you could do if you were one of their peasants. Shooting one of the king's deer, for example, was a crime punishable by death (or worse).

Though the punishment may not have been as severe, cutting firewood from a ruler's forest was also forbidden. Unless, that is, the wood was already on the ground, blown down by the wind. Then it could be freely gathered—hence the term "windfall" for an unexpected gain.

If you're lucky, you'll probably experience one or more financial windfalls in your life. Maybe an unexpectedly large tax refund; a bonus for some special job performed; money that you get as a gift, an inheritance, something along those lines.

So what should you do with it? Keeping in mind the idea of "paying yourself first," when you get these extra boosts of cash that were not part of your budget, you have an excellent opportunity to do one of two things: Build or rebuild your cash-reserve accounts, or put the money into your rainy-day fund, if you don't have at least three to six months set aside.

If you do have three months set aside, make an extra payment or two on one or more of your credit cards. It sounds so "common sense," but as they say, common sense is the most uncommon thing.

Whenever you find unexpected cash, think first of your Master Plan. Think about where would be the best place to use those funds to achieve your goals. Sure, take some of it and treat yourself. But don't blow it all on something frivolous. Think of it instead of the hand of Fate reaching down to give you a boost, and use the bulk of it to pay down debt and to build your cash-reserve funds and rainy-day fund.

"Winning is crucial to my retirement plans."

Start Saving Now!

As we conclude this chapter about saving for retirement, we can't help but wonder: Will anything we've said "stick?" Will it motivate you to start saving *now?*

We're concerned about folks in their 30s and 40s who are in denial about how much money they'll need decades from now when they retire. But we're particularly concerned about young men and women in their 20s who have no clue about the magical power of time and compound interest.

"Let's see, do I go to the beach with my friends for the weekend, or should I put $100 into my rainy-day fund or retirement account? Gee, let me think... I think.... *party! party!*"

Our message is that you can have your party weekends *and* save for the future. The key to doing both is to plan. Everyone was young once, so everyone knows that all parties don't "yield" the same amount of fun. (You can tell we're bankers.) So maybe you're more selective. Maybe you go to fewer but better party weekends and put away the money you would have spent on the duds.

As with every other aspect of this system, it's all a matter of changing your thinking. And making sure that you don't leave things to chance.

We know that many readers don't consider the philosophers of ancient Athens. But their advice is still rock-solid as a way of living your life today: *All things in moderation.*

The Power of Tithing

A close corollary to the principle of paying yourself first is the principle of tithing, which means giving 10% of your after-tax income to charity.

The Biblical principle of tithing has its origins in agrarian society, when the first 10% of the harvest was offered back in thanksgiving for good fortune of a bountiful harvest. The "first fruits" of the harvest were shared with those less fortunate, and in those times, the synagogue acted as a social-service agency to redistribute the first fruits to those in the community who were in need.

Today, in our post-industrial society, wages, tips, dividends, and realized capital gains are the bounty of our work efforts. So rather than offering the first 10% of fruits and grains, we have the opportunity to share a part of our income.

Chris Oliver helped us understand the importance of tithing. We began modestly, with 1% or 2% of our income—which at the time seemed like a lot of money for a couple struggling with debt—and steadily increased the percentage until we reached, and then eventually surpassed, the 10% goal.

Tithing is part of our Master Plan, and we support our church, food banks, and homeless shelters as part of what it means to us to pay ourselves first.

Many people follow the 10-10-80 plan:

- Give the first 10% to charity.

- Save the next 10% for your retirement.

- Live off of 80% of your income.

Principle 7:
Live Within Your Means

S ome years ago a man we'll call "George" died leaving his widow with a rather large surprise. We knew the family, so we were privy to a few details.

George was a machinist at the Philadelphia Navy Yard, the place with all the mothballed ships you pass on your way out to the airport. He spent his life turning parts on a metal lathe to incredible precisions—and he didn't even need a micrometer to check his measurements. He did it all by sight.

As a skilled craftsman, George made a good wage, with good benefits. But what no one knew, not even his wife, was that George was a real saver. He not only lived *within* his means, he lived *below* them.

That's how it happened that, when George died, his wife learned that he had willed her $1.6 million in CDs that he had established and funded over many years. The CDs were with several area banks, because George knew all about FDIC insurance limits.

> *"George was a real saver. He not only lived* within *his means, he lived* below *them. That's how it happened that, when George died, his wife learned that he had willed her $1.6 million in CDs...."*

You Can Do It, Too!

C an you do this? Sure you can. And given today's medical science, you'll probably live a lot longer than George.

Should you strive for a similarly spectacular savings goal? That's up to you.

Our point is not for you to amass "extreme savings," impressive as it is. No, what we want to communicate is the fact that you really can live within—and even below—your means.

As Kris says, it's all about being creative in how you spend your money. Or, to put it another way: *Think!*

How To Be A Creative Spender

Here's a simple example of creative spending: Never buy toothpaste without a coupon. Take the dollar you'll save using the coupon and put it into one of the savings accounts we've talked about. You sacrifice nothing, since toothpastes are all pretty much the same anyway.

Most Popular Splurges

According to a recent study by the Pew Research Center, people splurge on the following items, in this order:

#1: Food and Restaurant Dining
#2: Entertainment and Recreation
#3: Shopping
#4: Personal Items

If you're really honest with yourself, you could be smarter about how you spend money on each of these things. As could we all.

Being creative about spending money definitely does *not* mean doing without. It means things like waiting until the product you want goes on sale. (As we'll show you later, courtesy of *Consumer Reports*, seasonal sales are highly predictable.)

Another good example: When you're in the market for furniture, take a look at floor samples. Yes, that kitchen table might have some scuffs and scratches on the legs. But if you've got kids or pets, similar blemishes will be inflicted on the piece within days or weeks. So why pay top dollar for a table that's absolutely perfect, but will only stay that way for a short time anyway?

In other words, "Spend smart!" Don't just go with the flow. By living within or below your means, you'll free up money to pay off debts, fund your cash-reserve accounts, and make contributions to your retirement savings.

Creative Spending Ideas

L et's talk some more about how you can cut back your spending and start living within (or below) your means. Many of the money-saving ideas presented over the next several pages come from our own experience. Some we've gathered from CNN Money and other Web sources, as noted.

Ultimately, of course, the specific money-saving suggestions and actual dollar savings are not the point. The point is to get you thinking about how you can become a more "creative spender," so that you can start saving money, which you can in turn put toward achieving your goal of financial freedom.

Food, Glorious Food!

Cut Your Grocery Bill

The first rule of grocery shopping is this: Never shop hungry. The second rule is: Shop only once a week or once every two weeks. The more often you visit the grocery store, the more likely you are to fall prey to impulse buys. And, if you can avoid it, never take your kids along, because you know they'll try to make things hard on you if you don't buy them what they want (usually because they've seen it on TV).

Since about two-thirds of grocery purchases are unplanned, if you typically spend about $600 a month buying food and household supplies, you could save $200 a month by cutting out unplanned purchases.

Eat What's Ripe

Out-of-season produce costs 20% to 50% more than it does when it's in season. To get an idea of what's in season when, go to fruitsandveggiesmorematters.org and click on "What's in Season." When the list of fruits and vegetables appears, click on any item in red type to learn more about it, including videos on how to select it and suggested recipes.

If you buy your fruits and vegetables in season only, you can save upwards of $7 a month. We would add that we're whole-hearted supporters of the "eat local" movement. Visit farmers markets and farm stands whenever you can. You'll save money and help provide a living to a local grower in the process.

Avoid Bottled Water

There are all kinds of environmental reasons for not buying bottled water, but here we're focused on costs. Instead of lugging those expensive six-packs and gallon jugs of water home from the grocery store, buy a filter for your kitchen faucet, or a filter-equipped pitcher you can keep in the fridge.

If your family consumes 12 gallons of bottled water a month, you'll save about $15 a month by giving up the bottle. And, you'll be helping the environment. Buying a reusable portable water bottle costs less than $15. This purchase pays for itself in less than one month and reduces your output of plastic waste.

Clip and Use Coupons

According to www.couponing.about.com, casual clippers of grocery-store coupons can save $50 a month. Aggressive, well-organized coupon users can save much more. The site notes that, "The average family spends $8,600 annually on groceries. Trimming 20% off by using coupons would save more than $1,700 a year."

Coupons can yield big savings on purchases for your family, and of course, they aren't issued for grocery-store items alone.

(We never make an online purchase without first searching for an applicable promotion code.)

Sign Up for Clubs and Customer Loyalty Programs

It seems as though every retailer offers a "discount club" or "customer loyalty" program. Some require an annual membership fee. However, most are free, like the "preferred customer" program at your local supermarket that gives you a key-chain card you can have scanned whenever you check out.

Doing so makes it possible for the store to track your purchases and total spending, and in return, they reward you with special prices on certain products, and store coupons you can use for future visits.

Coupons Online!

Newspaper coupon circulars are likely to be with us for some time to come. But like everything else, coupons are moving to the Internet.

Here are four good sites to check for money-saving coupons:

Groceries: CouponMom.com
Online Shopping: CouponCabin.com
Free Shipping: FreeShipping.org
Cash Back: Extrabux.com

For online purchases, these sites offer coupon codes posted by users:

Retailmenot.com
Naughtycodes.com

If you're a Twitter user, here are five "tweet streams" you can follow for alerts on bargains and special offers:

Music: @amazonmp3
Travel: @JetBlueCheeps
Fashion/Beauty: @DealDivine
General Retail: @DealsPlus
Giveaways: @fstimes

Telephone and Cable TV

Consider a "3-for-One" Package Deal

In our area, Comcast and Verizon are the major Internet, telephone, and cable-TV providers. Both companies offer a "3-for-one" package deal to provide all three services for a single monthly price that may be less than what you're currently paying.

The deals seem to vary from month to month and from one location to the next. But the point is, wherever you live, and whatever companies you have to choose from, it's worth checking with each one to see if you can save money with a package deal.

And, since the telecom and cable companies are constantly battling for market share, you might get a deal by calling your current provider and telling them that you're considering switching to their competitor. They might offer you a temporary reduction to entice you to stay with them.

Cut Back On Premium TV Options

We would also suggest that you consider what you're paying for your "on-demand" entertainment and see if there might be some potential cost savings there. The question is this: Do you *really* need to be able to view the latest HBO and Showtime movies and TV shows the moment they become available on those services?

What if you were to cancel those subscriptions and wait a few weeks or months until the same programs are offered on Netflix (www.netflix.com), the mail-order entertainment rental company, or at a Redbox kiosk that you're likely to find at your local grocery story renting movies for $1.00 a day?

Also, don't forget that both Comcast and Verizon have "free" on-demand movie and TV-show offerings. At this writing Verizon charges $5.99 a month for unlimited downloads from the Starz Play library of 2,500 titles. Comcast offers a rotating selection of about 40 free movies each month as part of a regular Comcast subscription.

And then there is Netflix's "Watch Instantly" feature. Sign up for a Netflix subscription for $8.99 per month. This is the least expensive unlimited plan. It allows you to have one DVD at home. But you can swap that DVD for another an unlimited number of times during the month.

Buy a Roku set-top box ($100, one-time cost), and you'll have instant access via your hard-wired or wireless Internet connection to over 17,000 free movies and TV shows. Other Netflix-compatible units include the Xbox 360, TiVo HD DVRs, and Blu-ray players made by Samsung, Insignia, and LG. Be sure to check Netflix for additional options.

Once you install a Netflix-compatible device, you'll also have access to 45,000 movies and TV shows from Amazon Video On-Demand, but the videos are not free.

What About Your Phone Service?

According to BillShrink (www.billshrink.com), eight out of ten U.S. families pay too much for phone service. And that's not surprising when you consider all the confusing plans and options that are available. Your inclination is going to be, if it's working, and if everyone in the family is happy, then don't mess with it.

We completely sympathize. But the fact is that by rolling up your sleeves and digging into the situation, you may be able to save a lot of money. The BillShrink site is a good place to start.

Cutting the Cord

We've mentioned this earlier in the book as a money-saving option: Drop your land-line telephone service. About 20% of homes have chosen to do just that. Household members use their cell phones exclusively. We think that percentage will continue to grow.

And what about your parents? Cell phones are so inexpensive these days that many adult children urge their parents to get one, if only for emergencies occurring when they are away from home.

If you're among those adult children, and if you're actually paying for your parents' cell-phone plan, consider putting them on your family plan instead. That could cost you only about $10 a month (compared to $30 or more a month if they have their own plan). More than likely, your parents would only be using the cell phone for emergencies, rather than running up a lot of minutes.

Commuting and Car Costs

Slashing Car Insurance Premiums

Car insurance is one of those things that you definitely do not want to "set and forget." That's because the amount that your insurance policy will pay you if your car is damaged or totaled declines every year that you own and drive the car.

At some point, like when your car is worth less than 10 times what you'd pay each year for collision insurance, you should drop your collision coverage.

Raising your deductible can also save you money. Changing it from $250 to $500 could save 7%. Jump to $1,000, and you'll save 14%, according to CNN Money.

Some insurance companies also offer discounts for having a safe driving record and for teenage kids who make good grades in school. Be sure to review your car insurance from time to time and ask about discounts that may apply to your situation.

Transportation Reimbursement Plans

According to Section 132(f) of the Internal Revenue Code, employers can sponsor a qualified "Transportation Reimbursement Plan." It doesn't cost the employer any more money, but it allows you to pay for parking, vanpooling, or mass transit with pre-tax dollars, up to $230 per month. Your pay is reduced by the amount you agree to, but that amount is not subject to either income tax or Social Security tax.

To receive the cash reimbursement, you'll have to provide proof of your expenses. Not all providers offer such plans, but this is definitely something you should ask your employer about.

Switch from Premium to Regular Gas

And, speaking of commuting, are you unnecessarily paying extra for premium gasoline? Check the owner's manual that came with your car. Even if the manual recommends using premium, switching to regular is rarely a problem. From what we've read, it isn't going to damage the engine. The most you'll give up is maybe one second in the time it takes the car to go from 0 to 60 miles per hour.

Remember, in a global economy, carmakers have to design engines to operate in places where premium gasoline is not available. Indeed, if you own a car that was manufactured after 1993, it probably has a built-in computer that automatically adjusts the engine based on the grade/octane of the gas you're using. And the "premium gas cleans my engine" argument doesn't work either. All gasoline grades now contain detergents.

Premium usually costs between 20 and 40 cents more per gallon, and it is much more profitable to sell than regular gasoline. (Gas stations typically pay 8 cents more a gallon for premium, but sell it for 20 cents more than regular.)

So by switching to regular, you can save a considerable amount of money over the course of a year, depending, of course, on how many miles you drive.

Change the Way You Drive

Three final tips on cutting the cost of your commute: First, slow down. Gas mileage drops rapidly at speeds above 60 miles per hour. Second, keep your tires properly inflated. Doing so can improve your gas mileage by about 3%. Third, empty your trunk. You'll need to keep your spare tire there, of course. But carrying an extra 100 pounds of nonessential stuff in your car can cut your miles-per-gallon by 2%, especially in small cars.

Join AAA

One of the best bargains going, in our opinion, is the $65 (or $105 for premium) annual membership in AAA ("Triple-A"), formerly known as the American Automobile Association.

Your membership gives you access to free maps, trip planners, and towing services should you get into trouble on the road. It also includes discounts for hundreds of products and services, both travel-related and non-travel-related.

How about a 6% discount on computer products you buy from Dell, or a 10% discount when you shop at Target? Or, save on your allowance by purchasing 10 packs of movie theater tickets for $70. We use Hertz for rental cars because we always get 20% discounts with our AAA membership.

The AAA fee pays for itself by using just a few of these money-saving offers, making it a great deal even if the car never breaks down! For details, visit www.aaa.com.

Tax Credits for Plug-in Cars

For plug-in vehicles purchased after December 31, 2009, a new tax credit applies. It starts at $2,500 and is capped at $7,500 for cars and trucks. (The credit is based on the capacity of the battery system.)

The first 200,000 vehicles sold by each manufacturer get the full tax credit. After that, it phases out like the similar tax credit that's in effect for hybrid vehicles.

For more details on this and other energy-related tax credits, visit www.energy.gov/taxbreaks.htm.

Clothing and Shoes

Cut Your Dry Cleaning Bills

Studies have shown that 65% of clothes that are labeled "dry-clean only" can be safely washed by hand or machine. So says Kathryn Finney, founder of TheBudgetFashionista.com. For example, you can put linens in the washer and hand wash most sweaters in cold water (including cashmere and camel hair). Most silks are hand-washable too. (Bold colors like brick red, deep brown, and navy should still be dry-cleaned.)

If you're concerned about hand washing clothes marked "dry-clean only" or don't want to spend the time, you can also cut your dry cleaning bill by transitioning your wardrobe to cotton and other fabrics that can safely be put in the washing machine.

Often, "dry clean only" clothing, especially wool, simply needs to be freshened and pressed. We use a product called "Dry Cleaner's Secret" www.drycleanerssecret.com, sheets that are tossed with the clothing into the dryer. Clothing comes out smelling fresh, and then we press it while it's still warm. This is better for the fabric; not only do you save money on dry cleaning, but your clothing will last longer.

Finally, when your dark silk and cotton clothing begins to have that washed-out, faded look, consider dyeing it to restore a new look. Kris has been dyeing one favorite black silk shell about every other year for the past 10 years. Just follow the directions on a bottle of Rit fabric dye.

Repair Your Shoes

There's no shame in having your shoes repaired instead of replacing them, when all that's wrong is that the heels are worn down or the soles have gotten a bit thin. Instead of spending $75 to $150 or more for a new pair, you can probably have both the heels and soles replaced for less than $25 or $30. And when you pick your shoes up, they will almost certainly have been professionally shined so they look brand new.

Energy Costs

Tax Credits and Savings

Check to see whether your utility company offers a free "energy audit" for homeowners. Or do it yourself using the guide at the official Energy Star site (www.energystar.gov). CNN Money estimates that you can save $40 a month by plugging energy leaks in your home.

While you're at the Energy Star site, be sure to click on the link for "Tax Credits for Energy Efficiency." That will take you to a table showing you how big a tax credit you can get (30% of the cost up to a maximum of $1,500) for buying and installing energy-efficient windows and doors, insulation, HVAC equipment, water heaters, solar energy systems, and more.

Cutting Consumption

Here's a collection of easy-to-implement tips that will help you cut costs for heating, cooling, and electricity:

- **Install a programmable thermostat** ($35-$50). It's absurd to pay to cool or heat a home or apartment when it's empty during the day. But in the rush to get to work or school, it's easy to forget to reset the thermostat. The same thing applies when you're going to bed for the night and are too sleepy to remember to adjust the temperature. According to *Consumer Reports*, a properly programmed thermostat can save you 20% on energy costs each year.

- **Switch to fluorescent light bulbs.** These bulbs use 75% less energy and last 10 times as long as the typical incandescent bulb. They cost around $3.50, but they'll pay for themselves in six months. Potential savings: $7 a month.

- **Put on a sweater, but don't build a fire**. For every one degree you lower the temperature during heating season, you'll reduce your bill by about 1%. So, sweaters are good. Fires are bad, because they suck the warm air out of your home and up the chimney.

Entertainment

Saving on Books

If you're a book reader, you probably already know that the zero-cost way to get your hands on a book is to visit your local library. Thanks to the brilliant work of people like Elliot Shelkrot, director and president of the Philadelphia Free Library for the past 20 years, our local area has one of the most robust book lending systems in the country. We all should take advantage of it.

Want to read a bestseller without having to put your name on a waiting list at the library? Get a used copy on eBay.com or Amazon.com. (Barnes & Noble's used book offerings aren't nearly as extensive.) You'll see hardcover books with list prices of $30 selling used for as little as $5. That's better than an 80% savings. We don't know how they do it, but some sellers offer used books for as little as a penny, plus shipping.

Zero-Cost (almost) Books via Amazon

Here's a powerful money-saving trick: Buy a book at a discount on Amazon. Read and enjoy it. Then resell it through the Amazon Marketplace for exactly what you paid for it. You pay shipping on the way in, but your buyer pays on the way out.

You will need to sign up for an Amazon Seller account, and provide the company with your bank account information. Your earnings from book sales (less Amazon's 15% commission) will be deposited directly into your account. It's a sweet deal, particularly if you're addicted to hardcover books.

Video Game Savings

Everything we've said about books applies to video games, too. A great example is Microsoft's *Halo 3: ODST* (List price: $60; Amazon price: $50). Within a week after it was introduced in late September, 2009, used copies were available on Amazon for $40.

Once you, as "the Rookie" in *Halo 3,* have discovered what happened to your missing teammates, you may be ready to redeploy your entertainment dollars. So sell your copy of the game as "used" and spend the money on a new "used" game.

Audio Options

Most readers undoubtedly already know this, but we have to mention it as part of "due diligence" when it comes to the subject of cutting costs: Thanks to sites like Apple's iTunes and its competitors, there's really no need to buy a music CD.

Not when you can download all of the tracks from an online source for less than you'd pay for a "record store" CD, and either burn your own CD or copy the files to an MP3 player.

And, of course, the bonus of the DIY approach to music is that you're not forced to buy tracks you don't want. You can create your own, personalized mix.

Pet Care

Pets are big business. Should you doubt it, you have only to visit your local grocery store, where you'll find entire aisles devoted to pet food, pet toys, and cat litter. The flip side of this is that pets can be expensive. Here are three ways to cut costs:

- Instead of paying for pet boarding when you go away, trade pet-sitting duties with other pet-owner friends.

- Save on grooming costs by taking Puff or Rex to a pet-grooming school, where the service will be free or heavily discounted (40% to 50% off what you'd pay a professional groomer).

- Cancel the pet insurance. We know. Pets are very, very important to many people. But with pet insurance, you'll probably pay a lot more in premiums than you'll ever save on veterinarian bills.

"It's such a bummer, but it looks like I'll have to work for the next thirty or forty years."

Saving Money on College Expenses

Obtaining a college education is an expensive undertaking and may not be the right choice for all individuals immediately after high-school graduation. To take just one example, successful completion of a union apprenticeship or other trade school program may be a better choice for some young people than perfunctory attendance and mediocre performance in college.

On the other hand, there are innumerable reports that college graduates earn more over their careers than high-school grads. Assuming you or your child are intellectually and emotionally ready to take full advantage of your investment in a college degree, let's look at some of the ways to save.

Tuition is the largest single bill you'll have to pay. But whether you're the parent or the student, it's just the beginning.

Here are three suggestions for saving money on other college-related costs:

- **Books**. Avoid the brand-new college bookstore tome ($100 or more!) and instead rent the title from sites like chegg.com, campusbookrentals.com, and others for 40% less. For best resale value, don't write in your textbooks. The advent of new electronic readers (Kindle and others) should result in reduced prices as more textbooks become available in rentable electronic versions.

- **Meals**. Most college students don't eat breakfast every day, if at all. So instead of signing up for the weekly three-meals-a-day plan (21 meals in all), go for the 14-meal or 7-meal option. If reduced-cost plans like this aren't available, consider opting out of the school's meal plan completely.

  For a lot less money, you can buy a microwave and a small refrigerator, and give the young scholar a food allowance.

- **Travel and Other Expenses**. Check out the Student Advantage Card ($22.50 per year). With this card, students get discounts of 10% to 20% or more on everything from travel tickets to dorm supplies to clothing, all from major retailers and brands. For more information about the Student Advantage card, go to www.studentadvantage.com/discountcard.

  A Google search on the phrase "travel deals for students" will also yield many money-saving options.

Use Only Your *Own* Bank's ATMs

Our hope is that you won't be hitting an ATM very often each month. But whenever you do, drive (or walk) to one that's in your own bank's network. Out-of-network ATMs will charge you $3 to $4 per transaction. Over the course of a year, that really adds up.

If you live in the Philadelphia area, the ATMs in WaWa do not charge service fees. WaWa probably has more stores than your bank has branches!

Another trick we use to avoid paying ATM fees is to use our Fox Chase Bank debit cards (for budgeted purchases!) at a retailer where we can get cash back on the transaction. Not only do we save the ATM fee, we save time by completing two financial transactions (the purchase and obtaining our weekly allowance) at once.

This is also effective when you are traveling and have no access to your local ATM network. Go to a grocery store or drugstore for a small purchase, and take your allowance in cash-back.

When Do Products Go on Sale?

The Internet and Amazon, eBay, and thousands of other online retailers have forever altered the "traditional" retailer landscape. Still, because of the dynamics of the marketplace, retailers tend to follow long-time patterns regarding when they put things on sale.

The reason is simple: Bricks-and-mortar retailers only have so much shelf space. So they've got to clear out the previous season's goods to make room for the next season's products. The result is seasonal sales.

If you want to replace your window air conditioner, don't do it in July or August, if you can possibly avoid it. Buy the new unit in February when prices are likely to be the lowest of the year.

Though by no means complete, the nearby "What's On Sale, When?" table offers some guidance on the best time to buy a variety of different products, according to *Consumer Reports* (November, 2008).

Save with Creative Spending

There isn't a person reading this book who can't find a way to save more money. We know that because we're just like you. Rule Number 1 is to pay attention to where your money goes. Rule Number 2 is to figure out how to reduce your expenses by saving some of that money. It's a technique we call "creative spending."

This takes some effort, as we are the first to acknowledge. But that effort will pay big dividends, as long as you redirect those savings into paying down debt and working yourself out of your current situation—and building a nest egg for the future.

Remember, your goal is to live within your means. Or even better, to live *below* your means. One thing's for sure: When your money is in someone else's pocket, it is not out there working for you by growing into a larger sum.

Share Your Tips for Creative Spending

What clever ways have you discovered to save money? Share *your* tips for saving and read others' ideas at the Fox Chase Bank Web site (www.foxchasebank.com). Click on "SAVE! America" in the "Special Offers for You!" section.

What's On Sale, When?

JANUARY
- Bedding
- CDs/DVDs
- Cookware
- Houses/Condos
- Linens
- Swimwear
- Toys
- Treadmills
- TVs
- Winter Clothing

FEBRUARY
- Houses/Condos
- Humidifiers
- Indoor Furniture
- Small Consumer Electronics (MP3 Players, Digital Cameras, DVD Players, etc.)
- Treadmills

MARCH
- Computers
- Humidifiers
- TVs
- Winter Coats
- Winter Sports Gear

APRIL
- Digital Cameras
- Spring Clothing

MAY
- Athletic Clothing
- Athletic Shoes
- Cordless Phones
- Small Consumer Electronics

JUNE
- Computers
- Indoor Furniture
- Small Consumer Electronics
- Summer Sports Gear
- Swimwear

JULY
- Computers
- Indoor Furniture
- Outdoor Furniture
- Swimwear

AUGUST
- Air Conditioners
- Camping Equipment
- Computers
- Dehumidifiers
- Lawn Mowers
- Outdoor Furniture

SEPTEMBER
- Bikes
- Computers
- Gas Grills
- Shrubs, Trees, Perennials
- Small Consumer Electronics

OCTOBER
- Bikes
- Digital Cameras
- Gas Grills
- Winter Coats

NOVEMBER
- Baby Products
- Bikes
- Computers
- Gas Grills
- Toys

DECEMBER
- Bikes
- Computers
- Gas Grills
- Small Consumer Electronics
- Toys

Getting Going!

Now's the time to start putting the 7 Principles of Financial Freedom into action. We'll begin with a quick review of what you've learned, starting with creating a Master Plan and continuing on to the 7 Principles. Then we'll offer the Financial Freedom Action Plan, a guide for what steps to take next.

Your Master Plan, Revisited

As you'll recall, your Master Plan is simply a list of objectives. It doesn't matter whether they're short-term, medium-tem, or long-term, or a mixture of all three. The key is to have stated goals right there in black-and-white, tacked to your bulletin board or secured to the fridge with a magnet.

Keep in mind that this is a flexible list. As you accomplish one short- or medium-term objective, check it off. Or better yet, move it to a new part of your list called "Goals Accomplished."

Other objectives will eventually take the place of the ones you've already accomplished. But because you've achieved financial freedom, the new objectives may be things you never dreamed of while you were enslaved to your credit-card debt and interest payments.

There are trips to take and experiences to have—all paid for in cash—that are simply not available to you until you break the chains of debt.

And you now know the hammer that's going to give you the power to knock those chains off. It is of course: The 7 Principles of Financial Freedom.

The 7 Principles of Financial Freedom, Revisited

#1: Make a budget and stick to it.

Your budget shows you where your money's going. This is your guide to spending. Creating a budget makes it easier to see what you can cut (or cut back on) to start saving money.

#2: Give yourself an allowance.

This is your personal cash stash—"walking around money," if you will. Giving yourself a budgeted allowance is the quickest, easiest way to control what you spend on things like commuter coffee, vending machine snacks, beer and pizza with the gang, and movies. The iron rule that makes it work is this: "When it's gone, it's gone... until your next payday."

#3: Restrict the use of your debit card.

A debit card should be used only for things like groceries and gasoline. It should never be used to pay for impulse purchases, like doughnuts or fast food or gourmet food items at a specialty store. That's what your allowance is for. Restricting the use of your debit card plugs the hole in your pocket.

#4: Establish cash-reserve accounts.

The purpose of targeted cash-reserve accounts is to free you from having to use your credit cards for things like car repairs and inspections, home repairs and appliances, vacations and fun, and clothing for work.

#5: Start paying off your debts.

While you're building your cash-reserve accounts, you continue to make minimum payments on your credit cards. But once the cash-reserve accounts are healthy enough to cover their targeted expenses, begin paying off the cards, one by one, starting with the one charging the highest interest rate.

#6: Pay yourself first.

As soon as you're in a position to do so, start saving for retirement. Getting started early is absolutely crucial here because of the way money grows over time. Above all, make sure that you contribute whatever is required to take full advantage of any employer match for your 401(k).

#7: Live within your means.

Better yet, live *below* your means. There are scores, if not hundreds, of ways to cut your costs without reducing your quality of life. You just have to be creative about how you spend your money.

Next Steps

Now that you've mastered the information in this book, it's time to put it to work for you in the real world. That's what the Financial Freedom Action Plan on the next page is all about.

You might want to photocopy the action plan and track your progress by entering the completion date as you finish each of the steps.

There's no time like the present, so let's get going!

Financial Freedom Action Plan

1. **Make a Budget**. Gather: calculator, pen, photocopy of budget template in Appendix (or printout of template at Web site), three months of financial statements, checkbook register, records of bills paid automatically, three months of pay stubs (and any other sources of income). Fill in current amounts.

   Completion Date_____

2. **Budget Cuts**. Review the Can't Cut, Could Cut, and Cut columns, checking appropriate box for each item. Draw a line through current amounts you can cut. Then do the same for the "Could Cuts" and write in new amounts next to them.

   Completion Date_____

3. **Budget, Version 1**. Add everything up. Subtract expenses from income. Anything left over?

   Completion Date_____

4. **Budget, Version 2**. Repeat the cutting process. Goal is to come up with savings of 2% to 5% of income.

   Completion Date_____

5. **Set Up Your Cash-Reserve Accounts**. Visit your local bank and set up your cash-reserve accounts. At Fox Chase Bank, a Certified Savings Counselor at each branch can help you.

   Completion Date_____

6. **Fund the Accounts**. Automobile Repairs and Inspections, Clothing for Work, Home Repairs and Appliances, Vacations and Fun, Tuition and Books, etc.

   Completion Date_____

7. **Determine Your Allowance**. This is your walking around money that you can spend any way you want to spend it, but when it's gone, it's gone until your next payday.

   Completion Date_____

8. **Start Paying Off Debt**. Begin with the credit card charging the highest rate. Make minimum payments on your other cards until you get that first one paid off. Then start on the next highest-rate card

   Completion Date_____

You've Achieved Financial Freedom! Now What?

Think of this part of the book as "post-graduate work." We hope you'll read it the first time through, and then set it aside and read it again two or three years later, after you've gained true financial freedom.

As we've said several times, your first goal is to get out of debt. Your second goal is to start building a rainy-day fund capable of supporting you for three to six months. Then it's on to socking away money for retirement.

But once you master the principles of financial freedom and have all these other savings projects in good order, the next step is to become an *investor.* Saving for retirement, of course, is a form of investing. But that's not what we're talking about here.

> *"No one ever made a fortune off salary and wages. (The purpose of salary and wages is to help us live day to day.) It's thoughtful investing that builds true wealth over time."*

No one ever made a fortune off salary and wages. (The purpose of salary and wages is to help us live day to day.) It's thoughtful investing that builds true wealth over time.

True Wealth

"True wealth?" What does that mean? True wealth means different things to different people. We happen to believe that there is much more to life than money. We consider ourselves wealthy because of our good health, our great friends and family, our freedom to pursue things we enjoy, and the like. But from a financial perspective, wealth means "enough money to handle any emergency and fulfill your wants and needs."

It means being able to launch your children's careers without a mountain of college debt. It means being able to put a substantial down payment on a second home (or even buying it outright, without a mortgage). That second home might be a cabin in the Poconos or a place on the Jersey shore. Or it might be a condo in Hawaii.

True wealth might mean being able to travel abroad every other year—without using your credit cards (except as a payment tool to collect the rewards points). Or, it might mean the freedom to take a break from your career to pursue an advanced degree in a field you've always dreamed about pursuing.

True wealth also means a worry-free retirement, during which you might have enough extra money to help your grandkids go to college or start a new business, or give generously to your church, synagogue, alma mater, or favorite charity.

True financial wealth is about having access to a substantial amount of "extra" money.

The Basics of Investing

So how do you get this "extra" money? The answer: You use the same miracle of compound interest that we spoke of in the "Money Myths" section of this book. You give other people the use of your money, and they pay you back your principal, with interest, over time. But in this part of the book, we're going to introduce a few new concepts that complement interest, namely *dividends* and *capital gains*.

Infinite Variations

Earning interest on principal over time is the essence of investing. But of course, infinite variations are—and always have been—played on this theme.

For example, suppose there's a company that's wholly owned by its founders. It has shown itself to be successful over a number of years. Sales are up. Profits are up. It's doing really well.

But now this company wants to take it to the next level. It wants to expand to open more retail locations or build more factories to make more and different products. If the expansion is successful, sales and profits will go up.

Stocks and Bonds

The company needs money—*capital*—to fund its expansion plans. There are many ways that a company can raise capital, but we'll focus on two:

- **It can sell bonds.** Bonds are essentially promissory notes (debt obligations in corporate finance terms, IOUs in common parlance). The company is borrowing money from people who buy the bonds with the promise to repay the principal with interest—at a set rate—in the future. You need to be able to trust the borrower (the company) to repay your investment, and it is the promise to repay that makes high-quality bonds a pretty safe investment. Of course, companies can run into trouble too. And if they do, they may curtail interest payments or even be unable to repay the amount that was borrowed.

- **The company can also sell stock.** Stock represents a proportional ownership interest in a company, hence we refer to stock *shares*, meaning that you own a share of the company in which you invest. Shares of stock are traded on exchanges like the NASDAQ Global Market. If the company performs well and investors have confidence in the future prospects of the firm, the stock price will go up. If the company performs poorly or investors have concerns about the prospects for future profits, the stock price may go down.

The key point is that the money investors pay for those bonds or those stock shares flows directly back to the company issuing them. So the company gets the money it needs to expand.

If things go well for the company, it will pay investors a dividend for each share of stock they hold. You can think of that as *interest*. However, unlike the money in your FDIC-insured bank account, the dividend amount (or even whether a dividend will be paid at all) is *not* guaranteed.

If the price of the stock increases substantially, investors can sell their shares for more than they paid for them. The difference between what they originally paid for a stock share and what it is sold for is called a *capital gain*.

Risk/Reward and Perception

You've probably heard this many times before: There's an inverse relationship between risk and reward. The higher the risk, the greater the reward.

Investor reasoning goes like this: "If U.S. Treasury Bills—widely considered one of the safest investments anywhere because they are backed by the full faith of the U.S. government—are yielding 3.24%, why would I invest in anything riskier if it didn't pay me more than that? The answer is, I wouldn't."

This is Rule Number 1 of investing. So if someone tells you they can earn you 20% on your money, year after year, beware. Why? Because while 20% returns on investment are possible, such returns typically carry great risk, and are not sustainable year after year. This type of promise may be made by unscrupulous dealers, as the victims of recent Ponzi schemes discovered to their dismay and financial ruin in 2008 and 2009.

We should add that the way the market *perceives* the risks and rewards associated with a particular stock or bond can also be very important. Financial markets are always about the future. So if an established energy company announces a huge new natural gas discovery, its stock will probably rise, even though not a single new cubic foot of gas has been recovered. Why? Because the market anticipates increased profits from that newly discovered gas in the future.

On the other hand, if a week later one of this company's competitors announces that it has found an entirely different but equally large deposit of natural gas, the stocks of both companies may fall. Why? A huge increase in the supply of natural gas means too much supply in the future, and that will lead to lower prices and lower profits for both companies.

The Fickle, Unpredictable Market

Or not. Maybe the stock prices of both companies will soar to new highs. Why? Who knows? When it comes to accurately predicting market sentiment, the answer is that no one really knows.

The only thing that's certain is that whatever happens, there will be no shortage of television, radio, and newspaper analysts and "experts" eager to explain it all to the investing public.

> *"Never take investment advice from someone who screams into a television camera for a living."* —Tom Petro

These so-called "experts" and the multitude of programs devoted to investing on various cable networks all promulgate the myth that, given the right knowledge and guidance, you, too, can outsmart or otherwise consistently "beat" the market.

Which leads to the last thing we'd like to say about the "experts." And that is simply this: Beware of the people you see on TV, hear on the radio, or find on the business bookshelf at Barnes & Noble who claim to be able to show you the secret to beating the market. Some offer sound advice on investing. Others don't. It is often very difficult to tell which ones are offering good advice.

Slow and Steady Wins the Race

Historically, the stock market has generated an average annual return of somewhere between 9% and 10%. There are bad years and there are good years but—over *time*—that's what the numbers show.

Can you earn more than 10% on your money over the longer term? Sure you can. If you're willing to accept more risk. You might earn 20% for a while. And then you might lose it all. There's a reason why Aesop's fable of "The Tortoise and the Hare" has resonated down the ages. "Slow and steady" really does win the race.

The modern day equivalent of "slow and steady" can be found in *index funds*. But to understand this investment, you need a little background.

No One Beats the Market—Consistently

Every year, the *Wall Street Journal* publishes its "Best on the Street" rankings of professional stock analysts based on their stock picks and the return generated from those picks. The top rankings are never the same. In fact, men and women who appear in the list's top slots one year may not even make the cut the following year.

These are some of the finest minds in the world with access to the finest, most exhaustive information and analytical tools. And not one of them can manage to be on top year after year. That should tell you something. It should tell you that no one—not even "the best of the best"—can consistently beat the market.

The Magic of Mutual Funds

M any decades ago, individual investors would put their money into a "portfolio" of individual stocks, which they would buy and sell as they wished. Many people still invest this way. But in 1924, a company now known as MFS Investment Management invented the *mutual fund*.

A mutual fund consists of a portfolio or "basket" of stocks, bonds, and/or other assets chosen by a professional fund manager. Such funds sell shares to individual investors, and those investors receive a portion of all investment income, like dividends, while getting greater diversification than they could achieve as individual investors.

Open-ended funds issue shares to anyone who wants to buy them. Share prices are determined at the end of each market day by dividing the value of the assets held by the number of shares outstanding. The result is the *net asset value* (NAV) of the fund. Sales and redemptions are handled by the fund company itself. Most mutual funds are open-ended.

Close-ended funds, in contrast, issue a limited number of shares and trade just like other stocks on a stock exchange. The limited number sets up a supply-and-demand situation. That's the reason a given close-ended fund may sell at a premium above its NAV or at a discount from its NAV.

Investment "Outsourcing"

You might think of mutual funds as investment "outsourcing." It's like saying, "Okay, I'm convinced that Silicon Valley and the whole high-tech field is poised for a growth spurt. I don't have the time or the expertise to know what individual stocks to buy. So I'm going to invest in a mutual fund, managed by a high-tech expert, and give that person my money to invest. I'm going to do this by buying shares in the fund."

Fund Facts

- The first mutual fund was created in 1924.

- By the late 1960s, there were about 270 funds.

- The first retail index fund was created by John Bogle in 1976. His Vanguard 500 Index is the largest mutual fund in the world.

- There are currently at least 8,015 U.S.-based mutual funds with combined assets of over $12 trillion.

Substitute "emerging markets" or "precious metals" or "small-cap companies" for "high-tech," and you're well on your way toward understanding the huge scope of the mutual-fund business today. Whatever segment of the national or global economy you want to focus on, there's a fund to meet your needs. In fact, there are probably several dozen such funds.

Load and No-Load Funds

There are just a few other things you need to know to cover the basics. First, whichever fund or funds you choose, you need to check to see whether it is a *load* or *no-load* fund.

A load fund charges an up-front sales fee of between 3% and 8.5%. (Usually, it's close to 5%.) This is basically the sales commission that goes to whoever sold you the fund. So if you invest $1,000 in a 5% loaded fund, only $950 of your money gets invested. The other $50 goes to the person who sold it to you. In other words, you just lost 5% before you even began. You don't have to be a math genius to realize that loads like this take a huge whack out of your returns.

There are also mutual funds that charge no load fee up front, but collect a 5% exit fee should you want to sell during the first year. (The fee declines by a point each year.) These are usually called *Class B shares*.

Another approach is to charge you a *level load* of 1% a year. These are usually called *Class C shares*.

A, B, and C shares are all loaded funds with different ways of imposing fees. A no-load fund, on the other hand, does not charge a sales fee. But it may charge purchase fees, redemption fees, exchange fees, and account fees, none of which are considered to be a *sales load*.

There's no benefit to wading deep into the weeds here. The point is that you should not pay a sales load when buying shares in a mutual fund.

Motley Fool: Never Pay a "Load"

The Motley Fool is an incredible online resource for down-to-earth financial information. Here's part of what Fool Bill Barker has to say about mutual funds that charge a load:

When a broker recommends a fund for one of her clients to buy, that fund will be in all probability a load fund, and the load, or sales charge, is pocketed by the broker and/or other middlemen as payment for the "service of helping you pick a good fund."

You should be aware that there is no real difference historically between the performance of load funds and no-load funds in terms of year-to-year performance. In fact, according to the latest survey by the mutual fund data analyzer Morningstar, even excluding the drag on returns if the load were included in the calculation, no-load funds actually have a superior record to load funds over the last 3-year and 5-year periods.

Let us repeat that. Funds that impose no cost to purchase have outperformed those that brokers pay themselves to find for their clients.

—Bill Barker, www.fool.com

Index Funds and "Buying the Market"

There are many people who like the "action" of the markets. Think of all those TV commercials: the e*Trade baby, Rodger Riney and his Scottrade helicopter, "Talk to Chuck" from Charles Schwab, and others.

The main way these companies make money is by charging a fee when people buy and sell or "trade" stocks and bonds.

None of them actively promotes trading. They don't have to. They know that there is already a population of people out there, all of whom fancy themselves "players." Their pitch is, "We know you're a player. So if you're going to trade actively, trade with us."

This is the same audience that the "experts" we spoke about before are appealing to. And it is huge.

Let us say it again: No matter how smart you are, no matter how much research you've done, you can't consistently beat the market. No one can.

Yet, we all know that there's money to be made by investing. And we know about mutual funds. So here's the end-run strategy for everyday investors: Instead of trying to beat the market, *buy* the market. That's precisely what *market index mutual funds* were created to let investors do.

Why Index Funds?

What's an *index fund*? It's simply a mutual fund that buys and holds shares that represent the market as a whole. It typically has no bias toward high-tech, or precious metals, or commodities, or anything else.

An index fund *is* the market. And, because they have much lower management overhead involved in running the day-to-day operations, index funds have very low expenses.

This concept was introduced by John Bogle, founder and former chairman of The Vanguard Group. He came up with the idea in 1975, when he unveiled the Vanguard 500 Index Fund.

The premise is simple: If you believe in the American economy's long-term prospects, you "buy" into it by "buying the market." The Vanguard 500 made it pretty easy to do this.

Of course, there will be ups and downs. But—over *time*—you'll come out ahead. This is a very good way for the average person who is not a financial professional to invest.

But, of course, Wall Street being Wall Street, no one was content to leave simplicity alone. Today, there are dozens if not hundreds of index funds.

Some, like the Vanguard 500 Index Fund, track the Standard & Poor's 500 Index. Others, like Fidelity's Spartan Extended Market Index Fund, track stocks of mid- to small-capitalization U.S. companies.

Recommended Reading

The Only Guide to a Winning Investment Strategy You'll Ever Need: The Way Smart Money Invests Today by Larry E. Swedroe. (Available for $18 or less on Amazon.com).

This is a good book to read if you're interested in investing using no-load index funds. The title has more than a little swagger, but the investing guidelines are sound.

We are professional bankers, not professional investment advisors. We cannot make specific investment recommendations. But we can certainly suggest sensible investment "themes." And for stocks, a major theme is no-load index funds.

Bond Funds for Diversity

A ll wise investment advisors will insist that you diversify your investments. That's because, being wise, they know that—over *time*—some stocks go up, while others go down. Buying the market with an S&P Index fund or some variation thereof is the ultimate form of diversity when it comes to stock-market investments.

But there is another level of diversity. In a word: *bonds*. As we pointed out at the beginning of this section, a high-rated bond from an established company is generally a safer investment than owning shares of stock. The only thing safer is a U.S. Treasury bill. (We're talking investments here, not savings, because the safest choice for savings is always an FDIC-insured bank deposit.)

What You Need to Know About Bonds

"Safety" is the first thing you need to know about bonds. The second thing is that, because of their safety, bonds don't usually return as much on your money as stocks. The third thing is that, while a bond will pay you a steady, guaranteed return, the sale price for a bond at any given moment varies.

The interest rate on a bond you hold may be fixed, but if someone else comes along and offers a bond of the same quality that pays a higher interest rate, the value of *your* bond, should you want to sell it tomorrow, will fall.

That's as far as this book will go into investing in bonds. The main take-away is that, in general, you invest in stocks for growth (with some risk), and you invest in high-quality bonds for safe, guaranteed returns.

Or as Tom likes to say: "Stocks for growth, bonds for income." The goal is a *balanced* portfolio. (See the nearby graph showing the risk and return for different types of investments.)

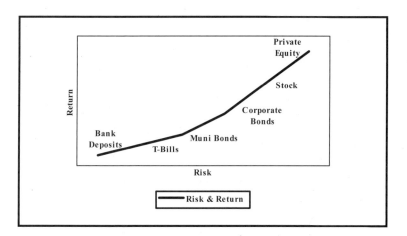

Portfolios That Track With Your Age

Returns on investments depend on the company involved. But basically, bonds and the interest they pay are a "sure thing." A given bond may drop or rise in its sale price, based on what percentage rate investors can get for their money elsewhere. But that's only important if you plan to sell or otherwise actively trade bonds.

The key thing about a bond is that its interest-rate payout is locked in. This is why financial advisors say that the older you are, the greater the percentage of your portfolio you should have invested in bonds. Why? Because bonds offer more safety and supply steady income that will substitute for your wages once you reach retirement age.

John Bogle of Vanguard has long recommended apportioning your investments based on your age. If you're 60, then 60% of your portfolio should be in bonds. If you're 30, then only 30% should be in bonds, and the rest should be in a portfolio of growth stocks or growth mutual funds. (Once again, the themes of "time" and "money"—and prudent risk—figure in.)

The Random Walk Theory

In 1973, Princeton professor Burton G. Malkiel published a book titled *A Random Walk Down Wall Street*. The cover art of this million-copy bestseller showed a page of stock quotes from a newspaper with darts randomly stuck by certain names. Now in its ninth edition (2003), the book's thesis is that you'd do just as well by throwing darts to pick stocks as you would by paying an investment advisor to pick them for you.

We highly recommend this book, along with *The Random Walk Guide to Investing* by the same author. Also the absolute classic, *The Intelligent Investor*, by Benjamin Graham.

Putting It All Together

To encapsulate it all: You buy stocks in the hope that their value will rise over time and that at some future date you'll be able to sell them for much more than you paid to buy them. (Dividends are also a factor, of course.) You buy bonds issued by a good company to lock in predictable, safe income.

We know any number of carpenters, plumbers, and electricians who have put major additions on their homes. Powder rooms, extra bedrooms, family rooms, and remodeled kitchens—you name it. In fact, Fox Chase Bank has provided many of these men and women with the loans they need to finance their projects.

Why? Because we had confidence that they knew what they were doing. They had the skills and experience to successfully complete the project and thus add real value to the house.

We would never presume to undertake such a project ourselves. We have the ability to develop a kitchen-remodeling *plan*, but we don't have the skills or experience to grab a crowbar and wade into the actual work.

So with this as a bit of background, why would you assume that you can wade into the stock or bond markets and successfully compete with the men and women who trade these financial products for a living?

So what do you do? The answer is amazingly simple. You put some of your money into a no-load stock market index fund. And you put some of your money into a no-load bond fund. Then you review your allocations at the same time each year and, as you get older, you move money out of your stock market index fund(s) and into your bond fund(s).

That's it. Managing your investments really can be this simple.

Dollar Cost Averaging

Dollar Cost Averaging is an investment approach by which you invest the same amount each month, regardless of the number of shares those dollars buy month to month. The concept is based on two principles. First, no one can beat or otherwise "time" the market. Second, historically, the stock market always goes up, earning returns of nearly 10% over time.

We won't go into the numbers. But the idea is that, thanks to the fundamental robustness of the American economy, if you invest some money every month, come rain or shine, you will make out well in the end.

Getting Help with Investing

We have some good news for you. When you get to this point in your Master Plan and are ready to take on investing, you don't have to go it alone. For starters you can call Vanguard (www.vanguard.com) at 877-662-7447. The great team manning the phones will help guide you to the no-load index funds best suited to your investing goals.

There are also a large number of registered investment advisors (RIAs) who are highly qualified at helping you build an investment plan and guiding you through the investment selection process for a fee.

Fee-Based vs. Commission-Based Financial Planners

Finally, there are many financial planners who are qualified to help you establish a financial plan and chart the course toward reaching your goals. But you need to recognize that not all financial planners are the same. *Fee-based planners* get compensated for helping you through the planning process. *Commission-based planners* make their money by selling you stocks, bonds, loaded funds, or insurance products.

Generally, we would advise you to consult with a fee-based planner. They have no real or perceived conflict of interest with you, since they don't have to sell you something to get paid.

Professional Designations for Financial Planners

There are several professional designations for planners, too. Chartered Financial Consultants (ChFC) are required to complete certain course work offered by the American College (www.theamericancollege.edu) that leads to earning the ChFC designation. The course work is rigorous, but there is no final comprehensive exam at the end of their studies to make sure they can integrate the various coursework into a comprehensive plan for your benefit. Some can. Some can't.

Many but not all ChFCs have an insurance-sales background and look to add this designation to provide a more holistic approach to insurance sales and financial planning.

Certified Financial Planners (CFP), on the other hand, complete rigorous course work and must pass a challenging and comprehensive examination. The CFP designation is granted and maintained by an independent board of directors whose mission is to benefit the public by granting the CFP certification and upholding it as the recognized standard of excellence for personal financial planning. (For more information, visit www.cfp.net.)

At Fox Chase Bank, we don't sell investments or insurance products. It's not our strength. Our focus is on helping people save and reach their dreams, and financing local businesses. So relax. When you come to us for help, we won't try to sell you these other products.

Invest! America

We've come a long way together from the burdensome old days when you were imprisoned by debt. Now you're on the cusp of starting down the path to building true wealth.

When you get to this point, ask around. Get recommendations from friends. But, please, be a smart consumer. True professionals will tell you right up front what they charge for their advice and whether or not they earn any commissions on the financial products they suggest.

We have also tried to counteract the notion, incessantly promoted by the financial media, that ordinary people can somehow consistently *beat* the market. What you *can* do, however, is *match* the market. That's why we have turned the focus on no-load index mutual funds and bond funds for small investors like us.

But we hasten to add that there are thousands of other ways to invest. That's one of the things that make market-based capitalism so exciting at times. Just bear in mind the whole risk/reward trade-off we discussed earlier.

Finally, we cannot say this often enough: If you are younger— in your 20s, 30s, or even 40s—you have the most powerful wealth-building tool of all in your hands: *Time!* That means that the sooner you start investing, the more wealth you'll have when you need it.

And if you are older—in your 50s or 60s—there is still time for you, too, since on average Americans are enjoying longer life spans.

But you must start. You must make the commitment. You can do it! Why not begin today?

Appendix A
Fox Chase Bank
Tools for the 21st Century

At Fox Chase Bank, we are committed to being a great bank for our clients, employees, stockholders, and local communities. Our commitment to excellence has inspired us since 1867.

For over 140 years, we have worked on being a company that we can be proud of. One of our core beliefs is to always act in the best interest of our business and family clients. We take a traditional approach to customer service: Simple and straightforward, with no gimmicks or catches.

We focus on being fair and honest with our clients, and we develop products based on client needs. We don't offer products that confuse our customers or attempt to take advantage of them. Our culture is based on a foundation of knowledge, truth, and understanding. Our employees are trained to appreciate our customers and to respond to them in a timely manner.

Being traditional does not mean that we are out-of-touch. We are continually developing new ways to make it easier for our customers to get information about their banking services, using proven technologies.

Recent developments, covered in more detail in this Appendix, include the ability to give your Fox Chase Bank accounts easy-to-remember Account Nicknames, Cell Phone/Email Notifications, and Direct Connect/Quicken for managing your personal finances. These are convenient, innovative, helpful solutions for today's time-crunched customers.

We also take seriously our commitment to good corporate citizenship. We are guided by the belief that the future of our bank is built from the strength and success of the local communities. Fox Chase Bank and its employees have a long and rich tradition of helping our neighbors.

Today, we support many nonprofit organizations through funding from the Fox Chase Bank Charitable Foundation, the Neighborhood Commitment Program, and through employee volunteerism in such events at the MS City to Shore Bike Tour and the United Way.

Old fashioned? Maybe. But we think that a forthright commitment to *truly serving* our customers is never out of style—and appreciated today more than ever.

To speak with a local Fox Chase Bank representative, or to find out more about how a relationship with Fox Chase Bank can help you, please call 866-369-2427 or visit us online at www.foxchasebank.com.

Setting Up and Nicknaming Your Accounts

In "Principle 4: Establish Cash-Reserve Accounts," we strongly suggested that you set up separate accounts for expenses like car maintenance and inspection, home repairs and appliances, clothing for work, kids' school clothing and supplies, and, of course, vacations and fun.

We'd like to make the case for setting up these accounts at Fox Chase Bank. You can open any number of accounts, with a minimum deposit of just $25. And there are no monthly fees.

Visit a Fox Chase Bank branch to set up your accounts and get your username and password. (For a branch near you, please visit www.foxchasebank.com/branch_locations.asp.)

Assigning Easy-to-Remember Nicknames

Once you've set up your accounts, Fox Chase Bank's Online Banking makes it easy to give each of them a nickname. For example you can nickname one of your savings accounts "Emergency Fund," or nickname your primary checking account "Bill Pay Account."

This makes it very easy to keep track of your money. Here's what to do:

1. Go to www.foxchasebank.com and log in to Online Banking.

2. Click on **User Options**.

3. When the User Options list appears, select **Change Account Nicknames**.

4. The next screen will list all of your accounts. Notice that there is a column for **Default Name** and one next to it for **Nickname**. Type in the nickname you want to use for each of your accounts.

5. When you're finished, select **Change**.

6. Finally, confirm your nicknames by selecting **Account Summary** from the Account Access menu bar.

Automatic Cell Phone Text and Email Notifications

At Fox Chase Bank, we're always providing new ways to use the latest technology to make our customers' financial lives easier. That's why we've rolled out our Fox Chase Bank Cell Phone Text/Email Notification feature.

Using this feature is like having a virtual assistant who notifies you of important personal financial events wherever you are. You can set things up so that you're notified via text message or email whenever these events occur:

Balance Less Than. Triggered whenever your account falls below a specified balance.

Balance Greater Than. Receive an update when your account goes above a specified balance. It's a great way to be informed the moment your pay is deposited.

Periodic Balance. Receive balance updates on your accounts. Choose from weekly, bi-weekly, monthly, twice-monthly, quarterly, semi-annual, and annual notifications.

Check Cleared. Specify a check number and receive notification when your check has cleared.

Maturity Date. Receive notification prior to one of your scheduled Certificate of Deposit account maturity dates.

Payment Due Date. Receive notification 1 to 20 days prior to your loan payment-due date.

Payment Past Due. Receive a reminder that your loan payment-due date has passed.

Personal Reminder. Schedule your own personal text reminder (up to 50 characters).

Setting Up Cell Phone Text/Email Notifications

1. Go to www.foxchasebank.com and log in to **Online Banking.**

2. Select the **Notify tab.**

3. Select the notification(s) you would like to receive.

4. To receive messages via cell phone, enter your cell phone text-messaging address in the email address box.

- **Cingular/AT&T users:**
  yourphonenumber@txt.att.net
  Example: 2155551212@txt.att.net

- **Verizon users:**
  yourphonenumber@vtext.com
  Example: 2155551212@vtext.com

- **Sprint/Nextel users:**
  yourphonenumber@sprintpcs.com
  Example: 2155551212@sprintpcs.com

- **T-Mobile users:**
  yourphonenumber@tmomail.net
  Example: 2155551212@tmomail.net

5. Click **Submit**. Please note that standard text-messaging rates may apply. Be sure to check with your provider.

Note: If you would like to receive notifications via email instead of your cell phone, simply type your email address in the email address box and click **Submit**.

For questions regarding cell phone or email notifications, please email ibsupport@foxchasebank.com or call 866-369-2427, Option 1.

Direct Connect Access with Quicken and QuickBooks

You can make managing your Fox Chase Bank accounts even easier with the bank's **Direct Connect for Quicken and QuickBooks**. Direct Connect gives you the ability to conduct transfers, import transactions, and make bill payments from Fox Chase Bank's Online Banking directly through

Quicken and QuickBooks Personal Finance Management (PFM) software.

Working with Fox Chase Bank's Direct Connect, these programs can help you:

- Sync your online Fox Chase Bank accounts with your locally based software by directly downloading balances and transaction histories for your checking, savings, certificates of deposit, and loan accounts.

- Transfer funds between your accounts.

- Manage and pay your bills using Fox Chase Bank's free Online Bill Pay service.

- Track spending habits.

- Analyze and report account activity using a variety of tools.

Fox Chase Bank's Direct Connect supports **Quicken for Windows and Mac** (versions 2007 or later) and **QuickBooks for Windows and Mac** (versions 2007 or later).

To get started, simply become a registered Fox Chase Bank Online Banking user. If you would like to use your software's bill-payment capabilities, you must also register as a Fox Chase Bank Bill Pay user. Once you've done this, you can connect directly to Fox Chase Bank through your software program's registration page.

Using Quicken with Direct Connect

Intuit's Quicken is the most popular personal financial software in the U.S. It's so popular that Microsoft recently discontinued Microsoft Money, recognizing Intuit's leadership in this category.

We've been using Quicken for years to manage our finances, and we think it's better than anything else out there. And, as noted above, Fox Chase Bank's Direct Connect Online Banking feature interfaces smoothly with Quicken.

Of course, you don't have to use Quicken to benefit from Fox Chase Bank's online features. But it's a great tool for putting yourself in control of your finances.

Which Quicken Package to Choose?

Several versions of Quicken are available at this writing. There is a free, online computer version, a free online mobile version, a Macintosh commercial version, Quicken Deluxe for Windows ($60), and Quicken Premier for Windows ($90). Premier includes investment tracking and management.

The free online version of Quicken is appealing as a starting point for managing your finances. But it has limitations. You must be online to use it, the amount of history you can import is limited, and it has fewer reporting capabilities.

If you want to be able to work offline and have more than three months' of historical information available, you'll want to purchase the $60 Deluxe version. Consider this expense part of your commitment to becoming debt-free.

Starting the Engine: Registration and Login

We are going to assume that you've bought Quicken Deluxe and that it has been successfully installed on your computer. Now you're ready to start using this tool.

We'll present an overview here. The documentation provided with your software and available online at the Intuit Web site offers much more detail.

Your first step is to get registered for your bank's online banking service. As part of this process, write down the user ID and password needed to gain online access to your accounts. Put this information in a secure place.

If you are a Fox Chase Bank customer and are not using Online Banking services, you can find information about how to do so online. Go to www.foxchasebank.com and look for the **Online Banking tab**. You may also call the bank at 866-369-2427 (Option 1), or visit a branch for help.

Creating a Quicken User ID and Password

With your bank user ID and password handy, go to the Quicken site (www.quickenonline.intuit.com) and create a user ID and password.

You'll be asked to provide the name of your bank. Select the bank that has your checking account from Quicken's list of bank partners. (Fox Chase Bank is a Quicken bank partner.)

A login screen will appear where you will use the user ID and password for your bank's online banking system. A list of your accounts at that bank will appear.

If you have multiple accounts, you can select one or all of them to be included in Quicken. Your bank transaction history will be automatically downloaded into your copy of the program and stored on your local hard disk.

You will also be asked to select the type of account from the drop-down list. Start with your checking account(s), since those are the ones that will be most important in determining how you spend your money.

Tools and Reports

Quicken provides a handy tool for tracking how you are spending cash. Using the **My Wallet function** will allow you to create records to track which categories your cash expenditures fall into.

Quicken will also attempt to list your recurring payments (utilities, mortgage, and loan payments) in the **Upcoming Transactions** section. You can add or delete transactions from this list to create a picture of your monthly budgeted payments.

Quicken: Assigning Categories to Transactions

The Quicken software will automatically assign categories to most of your recent transactions, based on the type of merchant. You can easily change a category by clicking on the Category field for that transaction and selecting a different category from the list that's presented.

If you need to add a category, you can do so by clicking on the Add button at the top of the Category column. Make it easy for yourself: Use the same category names in Quicken as the ones you created for your budget.

If Quicken is not able to automatically determine the correct category for a transaction, the words "choose a category" will appear in bold in the Category column. Simply click on those words to reveal the list of available categories. Scroll down the list until you find the one that you want to assign to the transaction and highlight it. The category is now assigned to the transaction.

The **Trends tab** will create a graph showing how you're spending your money. After entering transaction information, you can click on this to see whether it matches what you've created on your budget form. If not, perhaps you've mis-categorized some transactions. This graph is an easy-to-see record of your total income, total expenses, and whether you are living within your income for the time period selected.

Keep your Quicken records updated by logging into Fox Chase Bank's Direct Connect and syncing up your files.

Many books have been written about how to use Quicken effectively. (Just go to Amazon.com or BN.com and search for "Quicken.") Our goal here has been to give you an overview of how Quicken and other personal financial software can help you manage your finances, and how easy it is to use with Fox Chase Bank's Direct Connect.

Conclusion

And here it comes, the only "hard sell" you'll find in this book. You have to put your money somewhere. Stuffing it into a mattress is not an option. We would argue that you simply cannot find a better, safer place to park and invest your cash than Fox Chase Bank.

The big banks *say* they are devoted to customer service. Certainly some of them are, at the local level. But we're both life-long bankers. We've been in on the focus groups and marketing meetings. The image of "customer service" sells if you're a bank—even if you don't actually deliver it.

Well, Fox Chase Bank does indeed *deliver*. We are safe. Sound. And secure. We had no need for TARP money in 2009. We, unlike credit unions, are FDIC-insured. And we have a long, distinguished history. Fox Chase Bank is also among the most technologically advanced banks of its size in the area.

We would like to be your bank. Please take a moment to check us out, either online (www.foxchasebank.com) or in person. We *know* you'll be glad you did!

Appendix B
Your Personal
Budget Template

As we discussed in "Principle 1: Make a Budget and Stick to It," creating a budget is the key to your campaign for gaining control over your financial life. The budget template presented here is designed to help you do just that.

But it's nine pages long. OMG!

Well, not to worry. This template was created to include just about every budget item we could think of. Some items will apply only to men, some only to women, some to young people, and some to those who are young at heart.

Here are two options for working with the budget template:

- If you do not have online access, you can simply photocopy the template presented here, fill in the items that apply to you, and ignore the rest.

- If you *do* have online access, you can download an electronic copy of what you see here in MS-Word, Excel, or Adobe PDF format. The Word and Excel versions can be edited to match your own personal needs.

To download the budget template in the format of your choice, go to the Fox Chase Bank Web site (www.foxchasebank.com) and click on "SAVE! America" in the "Special Offers for You!" section.

Whichever option you choose, you can refer to the instructions in the "Principle 1: Make a Budget" section of this book for help in creating your personal budget.

Budget Template

Sources of Income	Monthly	Annual
Take-Home Pay		
Child Support/Alimony		
Investment Income		
Part-time Job		
Rents on Property You Own		
Online Auctions/Flea Markets		
Other		
Grand Total Income		

Your Monthly Expenses	Can't Cut	Could Cut	Cut!	Total
(Note: Use checkmarks or Xs for the "Cut" columns.)				
Home				
Mortgage/Rent				
Property Taxes				
Home/Renters Insurance				
Household Supplies (non-food)				
Furniture and Decorating				
Landscaping and Tree Work				
Lawn Mowing				
Services (Cleaning Person/Handyman)				

Your Monthly Expenses	Can't Cut	Could Cut	Cut!	Total
Home Improvement				
Maintenance/Repair Materials (DIY Projects)				
Other				
Home Total				
Utilities				
Oil/Gas				
Electric				
Water				
Sewer				
Garbage Collection				
Telephone (land line)				
Cell Phone				
Cable/Satellite TV Service				
Internet Service Provider				
Utilities Total				
Transportation				
Car Payment-1				
Car Payment-2				
Motorcycle Payment				
Boat Payment/Winter Storage and Marina Fees				
Insurance				
Registration(s)				

Your Monthly Expenses	Can't Cut	Could Cut	Cut!	Total
Car Inspection(s)				
Gasoline				
Maintenance (oil/lube)				
Repairs				
Tolls				
Public Transportation				
Transportation Total				
Food				
Groceries				
Dinner Out				
Take-out Meals				
Lunch (weekdays)				
Lunch (weekends)				
Beer, Wine, and Alcohol				
Other				
Food Total				
Clothing				
Coats/Jackets				
Business Wear				
Sportswear				
Lingerie and Underwear				
Socks and Stockings				
Shoes				

Your Monthly Expenses	Can't Cut	Could Cut	Cut!	Total
Purses/Accessories				
Jewelry				
Dry Cleaning				
Alterations				
Other				
Clothing Total				
Personal Grooming				
Haircuts/Hair Care				
Massages/Body Work				
Spa Treatments				
Health Club/YMCA/Yoga				
Manicures/Pedicures				
Facials/Skin Care				
Cosmetics				
Other				
Personal Grooming Total				
Health Care				
Health Insurance				
Long-Term Care Insurance				
Prescriptions				
Non-prescription Meds				
Doctor Visits				
Dentist				

Your Monthly Expenses	Can't Cut	Could Cut	Cut!	Total
Glasses/Contacts				
Therapy				
Vitamins/Nutritional Supplements				
Other				
Health Care Total				
Entertainment				
CDs and DVDs				
Movies at Theater				
Movies Rented				
Theater/Concerts				
Sporting Events				
Magazines/Newspapers				
Books				
Hobbies				
Parties/Holidays				
Other				
Entertainment Total				
Children				
Child Care/Babysitting				
Clothes				
Allowance				
Toys				
School Tuition/Fees				

Your Monthly Expenses	Can't Cut	Could Cut	Cut!	Total
Books/School Supplies				
Music Lessons				
Band/Sports Uniforms and Equipment				
Camp Fees				
Other				
Children Total				
Pets				
Pet Food & Supplies				
Vet Bills				
Pet Grooming				
Dog-walking Service				
Other				
Pets Total				
Vacation/Travel				
Language Lessons				
Airfare/Transportation				
Taxis/Buses/Rail/Toll				
Lodging				
Meals				
Excursions				
Entertainment				
Souvenirs				
Vacation/Travel Total				

Your Monthly Expenses	Can't Cut	Could Cut	Cut!	Total
Gifts				
Holidays				
Birthdays				
Weddings/Anniversaries				
Graduations				
Cards (all occasions)				
Charitable Contributions				
Other				
Gifts Total				
Education/Professional Training				
Tuition/Fees				
Books/Supplies				
Other				
Education Total				
Life/Disability Insurance				
Life Insurance				
Disability Insurance				
Insurance Total				
Home Office/Business				
Computer Equipment				
Printer Supplies (toner, ink, paper)				
Software and Upgrades				
Postage and Shipping				

Your Monthly Expenses	Can't Cut	Could Cut	Cut!	Total
eBay and Similar Commissions				
Bank Fees				
Credit-Card Merchant Fees				
Professional Services (lawyer, accountant)				
Business Insurance				
Other				
Home Office Total				
Investment and Savings (Current)				
Periodic Savings Amount				
Monthly Savings Amount				
Investments Amount				
Invest/Savings Total				
Personal Allowance and Cash Reserve Accounts (To Be Added Later)				
Personal Allowance-1				
Personal Allowance-2				
Cash Reserve Accounts				

Your Monthly Expenses	Can't Cut	Could Cut	Cut!	Total
Debt Repayment				
[List debts]				
Debt Repayment Total				
Miscellaneous				
Miscellaneous Total				
Grand Total Expenses				

Index